The
JEWISH
WEDDING BOOK

The
JEWISH
WEDDING BOOK

A Practical Guide to the Traditions
and Social Customs of the Jewish Wedding

Lilly S. Routtenberg

&

Ruth R. Seldin

SCHOCKEN BOOKS • NEW YORK

Grateful acknowledgment is made to the following for permission to reprint selections included in this book:

Central Conference of American Rabbis for the "Public Prayer for the Betrothed" in Chapter VIII, from the *Rabbi's Manual*, Revised Edition, 1961.

The Rabbinical Assembly for the marriage service in Chapter V and for the prayers recited by the bride and groom at the "Veiling of the Bride" ceremony in Chapter VIII, from the *Rabbinical Assembly Manual*, edited by Rabbi Isador Signer, 1952.

Library of Congress Catalog Card Number 67-13723
ISBN 0-8052-0186-6

Manufactured in the United States of America

First Schocken paperback edition published in 1968

9

FOR *Alex* AND *Yael*

Contents

Acknowledgments

We owe a debt of gratitude to many kind friends and acquaintances who offered encouragement and assistance throughout the writing of this book. Our special thanks go to Mrs. S. Gershon Levi, Mrs. Hertzel Fishman, Rabbi Philip Goodman of the National Jewish Welfare Board, and Mrs. Goodman, Mrs. Avram J. Twersky, Mrs. M. N. Fineberg, Rabbi Jerome R. Malino of Danbury, Connecticut, Rabbi George B. Lieberman of Rockville Centre, New York, Rabbi Gilbert Klaperman of Lawrence, New York, Rabbi Jeshaia Schnitzer of Montclair, New Jersey, and to the many rabbis throughout the country who took time out from busy schedules to answer our numerous questions. We express appreciation, too, to Mr. Samuel Mayer of Victor Mayer Caterers, to Mrs. Carl Horowitz of Hamilton Photographers, and to Mrs. John J. Stavery of Blossom Heath Florists.

We are deeply grateful to Hazzan Max Wohlberg of Malverne, New York, who guided us and who compiled the list of suggested musical compositions for the marriage ceremony. Grateful acknowledgment is made, as well, to Hazzan Ben Belfer of Rockville Centre, New York, and to Hazzan Charles Davidson of Elkins Park, Pennsylvania, for their interest and assistance.

For permission to reproduce wedding invitations and announcements, we wish to thank Mr. and Mrs. Joseph Lissberger, Mr. and Mrs. Haskell Zabitsky, Rabbi and Mrs. Isaac Klein, Rabbi and Mrs. Morton Leifman, and Dr. and Mrs. Don Levi.

A special measure of gratitude is reserved for Alice Rice Cook, whose lessons will always serve as an inspiration.

Above all, we thank our husbands and families, who are a never-failing source of inspiration and help.

Preface

The essential Jewish wedding has remained intact through-out many centuries of Judaism's geographic dislocation and historic change. In the course of a long history, Jews have lived—and continue to live—in every country on the globe. Wherever they have made their homes, they have incorporated customs and practices of that land with their earlier traditions. But the funda-mental elements of their faith remain untouched by time or locale.

A Jewish wedding may look different in different settings. The place, the clothes, the food, the festivities before and after, and the music vary greatly from country to country or continent to continent. And yet, whether the wedding takes place in New York, London, Buenos Aires, Tunis, Tel Aviv, or Teheran, the core of Jewish practice is always apparent.

This book is concerned with the American-Jewish wedding, which can best be described as a fine blending of Jewish rituals and traditions with the prevailing customs of American society. It is our intention to clear up the confusion and misunderstanding that do exist concerning the wedding, particularly those concepts relating to Jewish ritual and practice. Too often people confuse the "trappings" with what is truly sacred and basic, and tend to regard many distortions and excesses as rites in themselves. Myth and misinformation abound, and fewer and fewer people seem able to distinguish the authentic from the artificial, the vital from the trivial.

This book was written for those who want a wedding that is in good taste, dignified, and in keeping with Jewish tradition. Armed with knowledge and with a sense of what is proper and fitting, any couple who want such a wedding can have it.

Our goal is to guide such people in their thinking, and to assist them in planning the numerous details that a wedding entails. We have tried to provide as much information as possible about the background and rituals of the Jewish wedding. The basic elements are simple, and beautiful in themselves. They need little, if any, embellishment. Taking into account the division of American Jewry into three major groupings, we have described the varying practices of Reform, Orthodox, and Conservative Judaism. Members of the three groups, as well as the unaffiliated, will find guidance in the accepted procedures.

The social proprieties involved in a wedding are a matter of concern to most people, and we have dealt with these in some detail. Certain procedures and formalities are considered standard in American etiquette, and for the most part these have been followed. We wish to make it clear, however, that the book is a guide only, not an arbiter of what is absolutely correct. Times change, communities and families vary, and we believe firmly in the right to the expression of individuality.

It is our hope that this volume will help the reader to see the essence of the Jewish wedding wholly and clearly and that it will prove to be of practical assistance in the actual planning.

L.S.R.

R.R.S.

The

JEWISH

WEDDING BOOK

I
THE
ENGAGEMENT

שימני כחותם על לבך

set me as a seal upon thine
heart. SONG OF SONGS   8:6

It may be out of fashion for a man to propose marriage on his knees, but there is almost always a definite and recordable moment when she says "yes"—or perhaps it is he who says it—and we consider that from that moment on the couple are engaged.

ENGAGEMENT ETIQUETTE

In contrast to earlier periods in which parents arranged the marriages of their offspring, today's young people usually arrive at a decision to wed completely on their own. This is a healthy development, to be sure, but it does raise certain problems, particularly if boy and girl have not grown up on the same block, or even in the same part of the country. Parents, understandably, want to get to know a future son- or daughter-in-law before the wedding day, for despite all the freedom of meeting and mating in our society, a mother and father still feel a strong sense of responsibility about marrying off a child. Among Jews, who are noted for close family ties, this feeling is particularly strong. The Bible instructs us to "be fruitful and multiply," and to this day a traditional wish extended to the parents of a new child is, "May you raise him (or her) to *Torah* (knowledge of our teachings), to *Huppah* (the marriage canopy), and to *Ma'asim Tovim* (the performance of good deeds)."

The engaged couple will also have good reasons for wanting to take a closer look at the new families they are joining, and all too often it is difficult to find time or opportunity. There was a time when people frowned on overnight or longer visits to the home of a member of the opposite sex, but if a boy and girl are dating seriously, an exchange of home visits for a weekend or longer not only will give them a good picture of each other's family, but also will provide new insights into the mates-to-be, as seen in their native habitats. For families that are widely separated geographically, such visits, even prior to a formal engagement, may be the only opportunity for getting acquainted before the wedding.

Emancipated and independent though women may be today, there is still an extra bit of concern on the part of parents of a girl who is on the verge of marriage. It may be old-fashioned for a

3

suitor to ask the girl's father for her hand in marriage, but it is both socially correct and just plain considerate for the prospective groom to have a man-to-man talk with her father. A father wants to be reassured about the young man who is going to take care of his "little girl," and will want to know everything about him—including how much he loves her!

When all parties concerned make an effort to know each other, learn to appreciate and respect the things they may or may not have in common, and are sensitive to areas of possible tension, they are establishing a healthy foundation for future family relationships.

JEWISH ENGAGEMENT IN THE PAST

Until quite recently, most Jewish marriages were arranged by the parents, sometimes with the aid of a professional matchmaker, a *shadḥan*. This had been accepted practice since Biblical times, starting with the Patriarch Abraham, who sent a special emissary to find a wife for his son, Isaac. This is not to say that there were never any real love matches or that young people could not take the initiative, but the final decision and the formalities were in the hands of the parents.

In ancient Jewish tradition, engagement—or betrothal—was a formal, legal act, and it was actually more important than the wedding itself. The young man proposed marriage not to the girl, but to her father, and negotiations were begun. Because in Biblical times the marriage of a daughter meant the loss of a useful member of the household, the groom's family had to pay compensation in order to secure a bride. Later, however, as conditions changed and men became reluctant to shoulder the economic responsibilities of marriage, fathers of girls found it necessary to offer dowries as inducements to eligible bachelors.

At the formal ceremony of betrothal, *eirusin*, a marriage contract was signed, and the couple was then considered legally betrothed. This agreement was considered so binding that it could be dissolved only by actual divorce. Following the ceremony, the engaged girl continued to live in her father's house until the groom was ready to take her into his own, new home, which was generally a year later. The wedding itself was the transfer of the bride from her father's to her husband's home. This was carried out with elaborate processions, great feasting, and general fun and merrymaking.

There were always exceptions to the rules, however, some of them notable. We know, for example, of marriages which took place against parental wishes, such as that of Rabbi Akiba, one of the great sages of the Mishna. Akiba, who started life as an ignorant shepherd boy, fell in love with Rachel, the daughter of his wealthy master. Rachel, in opposition to her father, loved Akiba and agreed to marry him secretly—but only on condition that he go away to study. Disowned by her father, she lived alone and in poverty for many years, until Akiba returned, a famous scholar surrounded by many disciples. According to the legend, the disciples mocked the old woman in tattered clothes who came out to greet Akiba, and he turned to them and said: "All that I am, and all that you are, we owe to this devoted woman."

Not every girl married a famous scholar, of course, but there were certainly girls who married poor men. If the groom could not provide a home of his own, it became quite acceptable for him to move into his father-in-law's home at the time of the wedding, and to remain there for a year or two, or as long as necessary. Sometimes, if the bride's father could not afford a dowry, this free board was considered an adequate substitute. Is this so different from the common practice today of parents providing full or partial support for a couple still in college?

TRADITIONAL JEWISH BETROTHAL TODAY

Among many Orthodox Jews, a formal ceremony of betrothal is still practiced. It is called *tena'im*, meaning "conditions" or "terms," because a preliminary marriage agreement is drawn up by the parents of the couple. The ceremony includes the breaking of a plate, which, like the breaking of a glass at the wedding ceremony, reminds those present that Jews still mourn the destruction of the temples in Jerusalem.

MAKING IT OFFICIAL

The agreement between a man and woman to become one, must soon be shared with the public. First on the list are the parents or the very closest relatives. Most etiquette books suggest that the groom's mother act first, and call or write the mother of the bride to tell her how pleased she and her family are to have the young lady join the groom's family. It is then customary, if the families live near each other, for the bride's mother to invite her *maḥatonim*-to-be to her home, at which time some preliminary wedding plans will probably be discussed.

This procedure is suggested, but it is by no means a hard-and-fast rule. If the groom's mother does not take the first step, the bride's mother may do so. What is important is that contact be established as early as possible, and in such a way as to make both families feel at ease.

If the families have never met, the bride's mother will certainly want to invite the groom and his immediate family to her home so that they can spend a few leisurely hours getting to know each other. If the groom's parents are not living, his closest relatives call on the bride's family.

ENGAGEMENT ENTERTAINING

Parties at which the big announcement is made are now rare, but a party given after the news is out is a fine opportunity for getting to know aunts and uncles, grandparents, cousins, and close friends. It is particularly helpful if the engagement is to be a long one or if the wedding itself will be very small. At this point, to help clarify who belongs to whom, it is a good idea for the mothers of the couple to prepare simple family-tree charts such as the one illustrated below. These are helpful for social reasons and for working out the table seating arrangements at the wedding.

Sample Family Tree

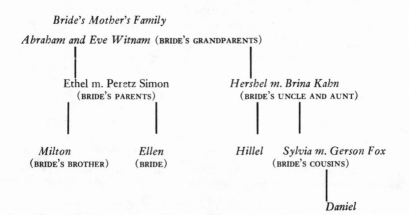

Bride's Mother's Family

Abraham and Eve Witnam (BRIDE'S GRANDPARENTS)

Ethel m. Peretz Simon
(BRIDE'S PARENTS)

Hershel m. Brina Kahn
(BRIDE'S UNCLE AND AUNT)

Milton
(BRIDE'S BROTHER)

Ellen
(BRIDE)

Hillel

Sylvia m. Gerson Fox
(BRIDE'S COUSINS)

Daniel

PARTY INVITATIONS

An engagement party may be given by either family and could take the form of a tea dance, a cocktail party, a simple at-home, or a more elaborate evening affair. Unless the party is to be formal, in which case printed invitations would be proper, invitations may be verbal or handwritten on note paper:

Dear Bernice and David,

Joe and I would like you to come to our home for dinner on Sunday, May 10th, at 5:00 P.M., to meet Susan's fiancé, David Katz.

We hope to see you then.

Yours,
Rachel

Dear Mildred and Bernard,

Our Susan has recently become engaged to David Katz. We would like to have you come and meet him at our home on Saturday evening, January 20th, at 8:30. Please try to be with us.

As ever,
Rachel

Engagement invitations can also be handwritten on a hostess's informals:

You are cordially invited to a luncheon in honor of David's fiancée, Susan Cohen, on Tuesday, April 15, at 12:30, at my home.

Naomi Katz

R.S.V.P.

Invitations that can be purchased at stationers are also appropriate.

Showers, bridal teas, rehearsal parties, and bachelor dinners are other forms of prewedding entertainment for which customs vary a great deal from place to place.

For Jewish families that are affiliated with a synagogue, a fine way to celebrate an engagement is to provide a *kiddush* following a Saturday morning service, shortly after the public announcement is made.

NEWSPAPER ANNOUNCEMENTS

About a week before a public announcement is made, close relatives and friends should be given the good news by phone or in a personal note.

If an announcement is to be made in the local newspapers, send the basic information to the editor of the society page. A simple, straightforward example would be:

> Mr. and Mrs. Joseph Cohen announce the engagement of their daughter, Miss Susan Deborah Cohen, to Mr. David Katz, son of Mr. and Mrs. Samuel Katz of Rochester, New York. The marriage will take place in June.

It is proper to provide additional information: home addresses, if both families live in the same city; where the engaged pair are studying or are employed; names of grandparents, if they are well known in the particular city. All this depends on local usage and on the newspapers' requirements. By all means consult the society editor, particularly if you want a photo of the engaged girl to appear with the story.

The announcement may be sent to the daily papers in the bride's and groom's home towns, to their local Anglo-Jewish papers, synagogue bulletins, and, if desired, to newspapers in a town where either family previously lived for any length of time.

If one of the bride's parents is deceased, the announcement is made in the name of the living parent.

> Mr. Joseph Cohen announces the engagement of his daughter, Miss Susan Deborah Cohen, to Mr. David Katz, son of Mr. and Mrs. Samuel Katz, of Rochester, New York. Miss Cohen is the daughter of the late Mrs. Cohen.

If the parent has remarried, it may be desirable for the announcement to be made by the parent and stepparent.

> Mr. and Mrs. Joseph Cohen announce the engagement of Mr. Cohen's daughter, Miss Susan Deborah Cohen, to Mr. David Katz, son of Mr. and Mrs. Samuel Katz, of Rochester, New York.

If both parents are deceased, the announcement is made by the bride's closest relative or guardian.

In the case of divorced parents, it is most common for the mother to announce the engagement.

> Mrs. Edelson Cohen announces the engagement of her daughter, Miss Susan Deborah Cohen, to Mr. David Katz, son of Mr. and Mrs. Samuel Katz, of Rochester, New York. Miss Cohen is the daughter of Mr. Joseph Cohen, of New York City.

Current practice also permits an announcement by both parents. Note that the divorced mother uses her maiden name, followed by her former husband's last name.

Mrs. Edelson Cohen and Mr. Joseph Cohen, of New York City, announce the engagement of their daughter, Miss Susan Cohen . . .

These are examples of commonly used and accepted forms, but individual circumstances may call for variations. It's all a matter of common sense and good taste, so feel free to be flexible.

Is a newspaper announcement absolutely necessary? Certainly not, particularly in a city like New York, where society editors exercise considerable selectivity in determining whose engagement or wedding announcements are published. Many young couples take a strong stand against newspaper publicity, preferring to keep the event personal. Their friends and relatives learn about the engagement in a more casual way. This is perfectly acceptable; after all, the news of an engagement is pretty hard to keep secret.

PRINTED ANNOUNCEMENTS

Etiquette has always frowned on a printed engagement announcement, but perhaps the times call for a less rigid attitude. Some families have friends and relatives scattered all over the country and in foreign lands, and it simply may be too burdensome to advise each one with a personal note. In such a case, a small engraved or thermographed white card that states the news simply (and has no resemblance to the actual wedding invitation or announcement) will gladden many a heart:

Susan Deborah Cohen
David Katz
Engaged   April 1966

These announcements may be sent by both families.

ENGAGEMENT GIFTS

The diamond ring has become the reigning symbol of engagement. To some minds the whole thing just isn't legal without that glittering piece of evidence. Whether or not you like diamonds, however, there is much to be said for the young man's sealing the pact with an important personal gift. For both the giver and the receiver, this gift acquires value far beyond its purchase price.

The gift from a man to the woman he loves should be a true reflection of his means, as well as something that she will cherish always. It may be a diamond ring, large or small, if that is what they want. It can also be a ring set with any other precious or semiprecious stones, a piece of heirloom jewelry from the groom's mother, a watch, a string of pearls, or in fact anything that has meaning for the couple. If it is a ring or any new jewelry, the prospective groom may be wise to take his fiancée with him, to assist in making a choice. If he wishes, he may visit the store beforehand and arrange for a salesman to show a selection of rings that are within a prestated price range.

In generations past, a Jewish groom frequently presented his bride with a handmade silver cover for a prayerbook or Bible, and there is no reason why this cannot be done today. These covers may be purchased at stores that carry ceremonial objects or Israeli handicrafts. Prices range from five dollars to several hundred dollars. If you can afford more, you might wish to commission an artist who works in metal to design and execute a cover just for you, making it as simple or as elaborate as you like, even incorporating small gems. Such a gift not only is an original and beautiful work of art that will become a family heirloom, but also has great spiritual meaning for many couples.

An old tradition among Jews is the giving of a gift to the groom from the bride's parents. A set of the Bible or Talmud, a beautiful *tallit*, or a fine *kiddush* cup are certainly appropriate. The gift may also be of a more personal nature: a watch or other kind of jewelry, a desk set, luggage, records, an art book, or something for the man's professional needs.

Engagement presents from other members of the family, or from friends, are optional, even if there is an official engagement party. (A shower is different, of course, but shower presents should be modest.) When engagement presents are received, they should be warmly acknowledged by the bride.

WHO MAY NOT MARRY UNDER JEWISH LAW

Jewish law prohibits certain marriages. If there is any question in the minds of the couple about the legality of their marriage, they should discuss it with their rabbi before proceeding with plans for the wedding.

The Bible prohibits incestuous marriages, that is, those between blood relations. These prohibited marriages are enumerated in Leviticus 18:6ff. In addition, the rabbis of the post-Biblical era extended the number of prohibited incestuous marriages to include relationships of a secondary nature and even beyond. A complete list of these marriages may be found in the *Jewish Encyclopedia* (Volume VI, pages 572–574).

There are other marriage prohibitions as well. A *kohen*, a descendant of the priestly class, is forbidden to marry a divorcée or a proselyte. Another prohibition concerns the childless widow who must obtain a release (*halitzah*) from her husband's brother before she may remarry. This prohibition is based on the Biblical law of Levirate marriage (Deuteronomy 25:5ff).

In general, Jews continue to observe the broad rules of consanguineous marriages developed by the tradition. It is interesting to note that the marriages of first cousins or of uncles and nieces are not considered incestuous. In a number of states of the union, however, the marriage of first cousins is prohibited, and Jews living in those states abide by the laws.

In Conservative Judaism, the rabbinate has relaxed the rule concerning the marriage of a *kohen* to a divorcée or a proselyte, provided he relinquishes all privileges and duties connected with this honorable title. The title itself, which is always handed down to the sons, is forfeited. Reform Judaism places no restrictions whatsoever on the marriage of a *kohen*.

Conservative and Reform rabbis generally do not observe the laws of Levirate marriage (*halitzah*).

Orthodox Jews for the most part adhere to the traditional marriage prohibitions.

There are a number of laws governing the remarriage of divorced persons to each other, as well as remarriage generally. Some of these are discussed in Chapter I X, "Special Situations." A rabbi should always be consulted by a widowed or divorced person who is planning to remarry.

II
PLANNING
THE WEDDING

HOW GOOD AND HOW PLEASANT
IT IS FOR BRETHREN TO DWELL
TOGETHER IN UNITY. PSALMS 133:1

Every little girl dreams of the day when she will get married, and many pleasant hours are spent conjuring up the magical delights of that far-off event. The same little girl grows up, falls in love, and becomes engaged. Then at last she has the opportunity to plan a real wedding, perhaps exactly like the one of her dreams.

The reality may present a few challenges, however, for a wedding belongs not only to the bride and the man she is marrying, but to their parents and families.

If the bride and groom come from similar backgrounds and similar economic and social circumstances, they and their families may follow certain established patterns, and the wedding plans will fall easily into place. But if the couple come from different backgrounds and places, there may be widely varying opinions about the kind of wedding to have.

Sometimes it is a matter of personality and taste. Perhaps the girl dreams of a large and lavish wedding, but her parents lead quiet lives and cannot see themselves as hosts at such an event. Or the parents want a large wedding to which they can invite all their relatives, friends, and business associates, but the couple want to be married privately.

The climate created by the discussions on this subject can have lasting effects on the marriage itself, as well as on the relations between the couple and their families. Unfortunately, the bride and groom are sometimes overlooked in the heat of discussion, perhaps because it is such a momentous event in the lives of their families, particularly the family of the bride. While it is customary for the parents of the bride to give the wedding, there is no law, either Jewish or civil, requiring the hand that writes the checks to wield the veto power. The wedding definitely should reflect the tastes of the bride's parents, for they are the hosts. But it will be a much happier occasion if it fulfills the desires of the couple.

THE COST

There are many things to consider when deciding what kind of wedding to have, and cost is certainly a major factor. In *The*

Catered Affair, Paddy Chayefsky wrote of an Italian-American taxi driver who was ready to pour his entire life's savings into a lavish wedding for his daughter—who neither wanted nor appreciated such a sacrifice. In the play, fortunately, the parents saw the light just in time, and the girl was married simply, in accord with her family's means. In reality, the same situation occurs frequently, but those involved are not always wise enough to keep the wedding within the limits of what they can afford.

If both the couple and their families want a big catered affair and the bride's parents can afford it, there is no problem. But such a wedding can cost thousands of dollars, and for many people may mean going into debt. Sometimes a sacrifice of this kind is undertaken willingly and with great joy. More often, it seems, people give weddings they cannot really afford simply because they feel it is required of them, even though it is not desired by the bride and groom.

What do the couple want and need? Perhaps the money to be spent on a lavish wedding could be more profitably used to help furnish a home for the couple, to pay for graduate study, or to enable the couple to travel abroad or spend a year in Israel. These questions should be looked at openly and courageously and the decision made accordingly.

Sometimes the groom's parents are in a better position to pay for the wedding than the bride's. This is a delicate situation, for custom has always considered a wedding the province of the bride's parents, who are "giving her away." It may be possible to relax this rather rigid approach, but only if it can be done with great tact, and so that no embarrassment is suffered by the bride or her family. The groom might offer to pay for certain essential items, such as the liquor, the flowers, or the orchestra. This could ease the financial burden without altering the basic plan of the wedding.

One suggestion for a groom's parents who may be unhappy at the prospect of a small wedding because they have numerous friends and relatives: a big engagement party or a post-honeymoon reception. Again, though, neither should be undertaken without first consulting the couple and the bride's parents.

None of this applies, of course, to a bride whose parents are not living and who may have no close relatives. In such a case, it is perfectly acceptable for the family of the groom to underwrite the cost of the wedding. If the bride has sufficient means of her own, she may prefer to pay for the wedding herself. This, too, is acceptable.

Following are lists of the expenses usually borne by the bride and her family and by the groom and his family. Not every wedding entails all the items listed (there may be, for example, no wedding ring for the groom), but the breakdown provides a general picture of what is involved.

Expenses of the bride and her parents

Engagement gift to groom
Wedding invitations and announcements; informals for the bride
Bride's trousseau and wedding outfit
Household trousseau
Wedding consultant or social secretary
Bride's blood test
Entire cost of reception
Photographs
Flowers for ceremony and reception
Flowers for bridal party, mothers, grandmothers, fathers, grandfathers*
Music at ceremony and reception
Rehearsal dinner or party (unless given by the groom's family or a close friend or relative)
Gifts to attendants
Wedding ring for groom
Accommodations for attendants
Gift to synagogue or charity in honor of the couple

Expenses of the groom and his parents

Engagement ring or other gift to bride
Wedding ring
Parents' gift to bride
Marriage license and blood test
Kiddush or luncheon following *Aufruf*
Fees for rabbi and cantor

* The cost of the flowers for the bridal party may be shared by the bride and the groom. It is not unusual for the groom to pay for the flowers for the bride, his family, and his attendants.

Flowers for bride and groom, groom's parents and grand-
parents, best man and ushers
Accessories for attendants
Gifts to attendants
Accommodations for attendants
Gift to synagogue or charity in honor of the couple

WHAT KIND OF WEDDING

Weddings lend themselves to infinite variation and to the
exercise of one's own imagination and taste. We generally think
of weddings as formal or informal, large or small, but within
these broad categories there is considerable latitude. It is possible,
for example, to have a very formal wedding with just the immediate families present, or to invite several hundred people to a
quite informal wedding. The ceremony and reception might be
held in one place or in different places; all the guests might be
invited to the ceremony and only a few to the reception, or vice
versa. Here are some possible variations to consider:

Ceremony and reception at synagogue
Ceremony and reception at home
Ceremony and reception at hotel, club, or catering hall
Ceremony at synagogue followed by reception elsewhere
Ceremony and buffet reception for all guests at synagogue or
    elsewhere, followed by dinner for immediate families
Ceremony at synagogue or home, followed by dinner, for im-
    mediate families and close friends, and after dinner, open
    house for other relatives and friends
Ceremony and reception at synagogue or home for immediate
    families, and large reception for relatives and friends at a
    later date
Ceremony at rabbi's home or synagogue study, which may or
    may not be followed by a reception

THE PLACE

In Judaism, sanctity is not confined to the synagogue, and
Jewish law has no fixed requirements concerning the place in
which a wedding is held. Many rituals are in fact performed
outside the synagogue, especially in the home. The rabbis of old

called a man's table a *mizbei'ah*, an altar, because blessings are recited there. If a man cannot recite daily or Sabbath prayers at synagogue, he is considered to have fulfilled his obligation if he prays at home or wherever he may be. What is important from the religious point of view is not the place per se, but the religious spirit permeating the event and the proper observance of the relevant laws and rituals.

In theory, a Jewish wedding may be held almost anywhere. In practice, however, most rabbis today consider a synagogue or a home the appropriate places in which to be married. Only a synagogue or a home can provide the proper spiritual setting for a wedding: a synagogue, because it is the House of the Lord; a home, because it offers the intimacy and warmth that should mark an event as personal as a marriage. It is not even necessary to choose the synagogue or the home of the bride's parents. An unfamiliar synagogue or the home of a relative or friend may lack the sentiment of long association, but they still offer the desired atmosphere.

What about hotels, catering halls, clubs, and the like? In large metropolitan centers, more weddings are held in such establishments than in synagogues or homes, because many people do not have access to a synagogue or are limited by the size of their homes. People often choose to be married in a hotel or hall because all the arrangements are taken care of by professionals. The customer has only to choose between the various plans presented to him, and can go home confident that all the details will be handled smoothly and efficiently.

But there are drawbacks. Large hotels and catering halls often book more than one wedding for the same date and time, and the result can be unfortunate. It is not uncommon for a ceremony to be performed to the accompaniment of a dance band at the reception next door. And it is not beneath some establishments to use the food and flowers left over from one event at the next.

Weddings are now big business. Somehow we have permitted the caterers, banquet managers, and other professionals to dictate the tone and style of our marriages. Professionals have their place, and most of us could not manage without them, but many of us seem to have forgotten that they exist to serve *our* needs and tastes. A caterer or banquet manager may have impeccable judgment in food, wines, table arrangements, and the like—but what about the preferences of the bride and her parents? If they have ideas of their own, they may have little opportunity to express them.

Equally important, the caterer or banquet manager is not necessarily qualified to determine what constitutes a proper Jewish wedding. This criticism applies to many official synagogue caterers as well as to hotels and halls, for, unfortunately, many synagogues have permitted caterers to take over the entire wedding, to run everything but the actual ceremony.

A wedding should be dignified, not dazzling. Colored lights, a spiral staircase for the bride's descent, Broadway show tunes, and doves flying out of gilded cages are completely out of place at a wedding ceremony, no matter where it is held. Many such sins against good taste are committed in the hope of providing an unforgettable wedding—and they would all be best forgotten.

One widespread practice that is being eliminated by a growing number of synagogues is the serving of food and drinks prior to the ceremony. By the time the ceremony starts, the guests often feel more like New Year's Eve revelers than witnesses to a sacred ceremony, and on occasion their behavior shows it. Jewish tradition calls for merrymaking at a wedding, but it should be reserved for the right time and place. Another objection leveled at the smorgasbord, as it is often called, is that it provides food to people who are going to be fed again, abundantly, as soon as the ceremony is over.

Choosing a Synagogue. The first choice should be the synagogue of which the bride's parents are members, the second choice the synagogue to which the groom's parents belong. If neither family is affiliated with a synagogue, or if their synagogues do not have adequate wedding facilities, the bride and her parents should select one that will best meet their needs in terms of their religious preference, available dates, the accommodations, the location, and the cost. If they are not familiar with the practices of a particular synagogue, they should ask permission to observe a wedding there. Later they may take up their questions with the executive director, caterer, or whoever is in charge.

Most synagogues make their facilities available to people who are not affiliated as well as to members. For the person who is not a member, there may be a comprehensive fee covering use of the sanctuary, and services of the rabbi, cantor, and organist, apart from the caterer's charge for the reception.

Choosing a Hotel or Hall. Though holding a wedding in a commercial establishment is often less than ideal, for many people there is no alternative. It should be stated, too, that many such places do provide beautiful weddings in good taste. Hotels may be preferable in this regard, because they usually leave it to the customer to decide what kind of wedding to have. Catering halls generally have fixed routines; one may choose between several plans, but there is little chance to deviate from the basic framework.

It is often wise to choose a weekday for the wedding so as to avoid the weekend crush. Arranging to observe a live wedding at the hotel or hall before making a decision is prudent. If some of the procedures are objectionable, perhaps they can be eliminated or modified. If not, the search may have to be carried further.

It is important to consider the number of guests when selecting a room or hall. There is nothing so dampening to the spirits as the sight of fifty or sixty people in a yawning banquet hall. Conversely, at a wedding for several hundred guests, there should be ample space at the tables and on the dance floor.

Small cities and towns have fewer facilities for weddings than do large cities, particularly if kosher food is to be served. If the place that is selected has not had much experience with Jewish weddings, it may be up to the hosts to provide the necessary ritual items (canopy, *kiddush* cup, sacramental wine, etc.) and to instruct the staff in the procedures to be followed. The local rabbi who is to officiate will be glad to offer his assistance with the arrangements.

Sometimes a wedding must take place in a town in which neither family resides. It is not uncommon, for example, for a young man serving in the armed forces to marry the girl he left behind, and to have the wedding in a town near where he is stationed. In this or a similar situation, a rabbi in that town should be called for guidance and assistance. A rabbi in one's home community can provide the name and address of a rabbi in the strange locale.

SETTING THE DATE

It is important to arrive at a date for the wedding early, particularly if it is to be held anywhere but in your own home. It is often necessary to reserve a synagogue or hotel many months in advance, especially for December and June weddings. If the engagement is to be short, therefore, the planning may have to be more flexible. Bear in mind, too, that the rabbi whom you wish to officiate may have prior commitments.

There are certain dates in the Jewish calendar when weddings may not be held, and for this reason it is wise to consult a rabbi before making a decision. The days that come into question are:

1. Sabbaths, Festivals, and the intermediate days of Pesaḥ and Sukkot: no weddings are permitted. Weddings may be held on Ḥanukah and Purim.

2. In the spring, the period of *Sefirah*, the forty-nine days starting from the second day of Pesaḥ and ending with Shavuot: Orthodox and Conservative rabbis generally do not officiate at weddings during this period, except for certain days. In Reform Judaism, weddings are permitted during this period.

3. In the summer, the three-week period from the 17th of Tammuz to the 9th of Av (*Tisha B'Av*). This is a period of mourning commemorating the destruction of the two Temples in Jerusalem, in 586 B.C.E. and in 70 C.E. Orthodox, and most Conservative rabbis will not solemnize marriages during this period, except in emergency situations. Reform Judaism does not observe this period, but some Reform rabbis do not officiate at weddings on the 9th of Av.

4. Minor fast days: All Orthodox and some Conservative rabbis will not perform marriages on the four minor fast days: the Fast of Gedalia (3rd of Tishrei), the 10th of Tevet, the Fast of Esther (13th of Adar), and the 17th of Tammuz.

Weddings are permitted, but not encouraged, by Orthodox and Conservative rabbis on the days between Rosh Hashanah and Yom Kippur.

Any day of the week, except Friday night or Saturday before sundown, is suitable for a wedding. Traditionally, Tuesday was considered a favored day, and Monday was thought to be unlucky. The explanation given is that in the account of Creation in the Book of Genesis, God concludes His handiwork of the third day (Tuesday) by twice saying, "It was good," but for the work of the second day (Monday), this phrase is not used at all. Friday, before sunset, was also considered an auspicious day, probably because the wedding celebration was then coupled with the festivities of the Sabbath, even though the actual wedding feast could not be held until Saturday night.

HOUR OF THE WEDDING

A Jewish wedding may be held at any time of day. The only restrictions concern Sabbaths and Festivals, which begin at sunset and end after dark. In Orthodox and Conservative synagogues, a wedding on a Saturday night or after a Festival may not begin until an hour and a half or more after sunset. This allows sufficient time for the caterer and florist to complete their preparations and for observant guests and the rabbi to travel to the wedding. Members of the wedding party and guests should be advised not to arrive at the synagogue until the concluding Sabbath or Festival services are over.

Many synagogues discourage Saturday-night weddings during the late spring and summer, because sunset is so late. Under such circumstances, dinner is usually not served until close to midnight, which works a hardship on everyone. Unless there is to be a simple reception, therefore, it is probably wiser to avoid Saturday night in the spring and summer months.

Evening weddings are popular everywhere, probably because they provide an opportunity for greater formality and the wearing of elaborate clothes. On a weekend, people are generally more relaxed, and the celebration may go on into the wee hours. One disadvantage of an evening wedding is that the bride and groom have a long day of waiting, and then may not be able to leave on their wedding trip until the following day.

A daytime wedding may be held anytime from late morning to five o'clock. It may be formal or informal, though it can rarely be as elaborate as an evening affair. It does have advantages, though: the bride and groom have a short day, and can leave at a reasonable hour; guests can expect to get home early; and out-of-town guests can, if necessary, come and go on the same day. If children are to be present, they are more likely to be at their best during the day.

WHO IS TO OFFICIATE

It is customary for the rabbi and cantor of the synagogue where the wedding is to take place to officiate at the ceremony. If either the bride or groom wishes to have a second rabbi and cantor participate, permission must be granted by the host rabbi and cantor. Generally, they will be pleased to invite colleagues to assist in officiating. The rabbis discuss the division of the service in advance, with the understanding that the final decision rests with the host rabbi.

Guest rabbis who are close to the families do not necessarily take part in the ceremony; they may be asked to offer remarks after dinner, or may be honored with reciting the *Sheva Berakhot*, the Seven Wedding Blessings, at the conclusion of the meal.

If the wedding is not held in a synagogue, any rabbi may be invited to officiate. Someone known personally is best, of course, or someone known well to a close friend or relative. Sometimes a hotel or wedding hall will recommend a rabbi or will suggest several.

If the principals do not know any rabbis personally or are being married in a strange town, they may call a synagogue and speak to its rabbi. If he himself is not available, he will suggest colleagues who may be called. In the event that the couple have definite religious preferences, they must make sure to ask about the rabbi's affiliation early enough so that there is no misunderstanding later on.

People often ask whether it is essential to have both a rabbi and a cantor officiate, or whether one is sufficient. At synagogue weddings, it is accepted practice to have the rabbi officiate with the cantor assisting. For weddings held elsewhere, the answer may depend on the laws of the state in which the wedding takes place. In New York, for example, any synagogue functionary, whether or not he is an ordained rabbi, may be licensed to perform a marriage ceremony. This would include cantors. Jewish law itself requires only that the person who solemnizes a marriage (*mesader kiddushin*) be a learned and pious man, well versed in the legal requirements of marriage. For all practical purposes, this has come to mean an ordained rabbi. Ideally, therefore, the marriage should be solemnized by an ordained rabbi with a cantor assisting.

FEES FOR THE RABBI AND CANTOR

Most rabbis and cantors do not have set fees for officiating at weddings. Some synagogues, however, have established standard fees for marriages of nonaffiilated persons and occasionally for members as well. The same may apply to a hotel or wedding hall that provides the rabbi and cantor.

If it is the rabbi of either the bride or groom who is officiating, or if they know him personally, they ought not to embarrass him by asking what his fee is. If they are uncertain, they may consult a member of the synagogue staff. If the rabbi is a stranger, on the other hand, it would be wise to inquire tactfully whether there will be a set fee for his services. When the rabbi is a personal friend, or has known either of the principals for a long time, they may choose to give him an appropriate gift rather than a fee.

If the rabbi is a relative of either bride or groom, it is customary to seat him and his wife at the bridal table, and to thank him for his services by sending him a warm note, and perhaps a gift, afterward.

When a rabbi has been invited to come from out of town to officiate at a wedding, his traveling and hotel expenses are paid by those who have invited him.

The groom or his best man may hand the fees, in envelopes, to the rabbi and cantor privately after the ceremony, or, if desired, the fees may be mailed with thank-you notes.

PREMARITAL MEETING WITH THE RABBI

The rabbi is not just a third party under the wedding canopy; he is as much a member of the wedding as the bride and groom and their families. If he has known the bride or groom for a number of years, chances are that he does in fact feel himself a member of the family. He is proud and happy at seeing the couple reach this milestone, and he is deeply concerned about their future happiness. Even if he has not known them long or well, he cares about them. By performing their marriage ceremony, he is helping to create a new family, and he feels an obligation to them, to society at large, and to the Jewish community to make certain that this new creation will be a happy, stable, and productive one.

The rabbi will want to meet with the couple, generally well in advance of the wedding, so a date and time should be set for this when he is asked to officiate. He will have a number of things to take up with them, but just as important, this premarital interview is their opportunity to discuss personal problems, if they have them, with a sympathetic and experienced counsellor.

No matter how deeply in love a couple may be, the decision to marry inevitably results in questions, and conflicts—with families, and even with each other—which tend to become magnified in the supercharged atmosphere surrounding the wedding. The rabbi's study is a quiet oasis in which to examine problems calmly and objectively. The rabbi can help to place troubling questions in perspective; if he senses areas of serious difficulty, he may suggest counseling, either by himself or by a therapist.

In the midst of prewedding plans and excitement, the meeting with the rabbi provides a chance to think and talk about the deeper significance of the new life the bride and groom are embarking on. The rabbi will tell them something about the Jewish view of marriage and the respective obligations of husband and wife. He will discuss the kind of Jewish home they are going to establish and their role as members of the Jewish community.

The wedding ceremony, its symbols and rituals and how the couple participate, is an important subject to be taken up at this meeting. They may want to ask about rituals that are unclear to them or to suggest certain practices for inclusion in the ceremony. The rabbi will tell them about his own procedures and practices or those of the synagogue where the ceremony is to be held.

The rabbi makes certain that the marriage meets the requirements of Jewish religious law. This is usually a simple matter to ascertain, but occasionally complications do arise. For example, if either party has had a civil divorce but not a religious divorce, an Orthodox or Conservative rabbi will decline to officiate. He will, however, offer his help in securing a religious divorce, so that the marriage may ultimately take place. Another example: if either party is the offspring of a non-Jewish mother, and thus not legally Jewish, almost every rabbi will require a formal act of conversion before agreeing to officiate.

For Orthodox and Conservative ceremonies, the rabbi will want to know the couple's Hebrew names and their fathers' Hebrew names. This information must be included in the marriage contract (*ketubah*).

Do the couple have a marriage license? Have they taken blood tests? Since the rabbi is solemnizing the marriage according to civil, as well as Jewish, law, he must make sure that all state and local requirements are fulfilled. If the couple are uncertain about these requirements, he will provide the necessary information.

The premarital interview is for the bride and groom alone. What the couple discuss with the rabbi remains wholly confidential, and the rabbi must feel free to speak openly and honestly. Wise parents understand this; they will not attempt to pry, and they will certainly not ask the rabbi to influence the couple in an area of disagreement. If the rabbi becomes aware of conflict, he will decide for himself how to deal with it.

III

Invitations and Announcements

זה היום עשה יי

THIS IS THE DAY WHICH THE LORD HATH MADE;
ON IT WE WILL BE GLAD AND REJOICE. PSALMS
118:24

There are two sides to the marriage coin—the private and the public. A man and woman about to be wed are very much in the public eye; only after the wedding will they be able to savor the delights of privacy.

A wedding means guests to be invited, others to be informed of the event by announcements, and the world at large to be apprised of the new union through the press. For most families, these are important matters, which call for careful planning and sound judgment.

You Have a Little List

As anyone knows who has once lived through a wedding, the trouble with the guest list is that it has a way of growing—unless you keep a firm grip on it. That is why it is so important for the hosts, generally the bride's parents, to establish clear-cut guidelines from the outset. As gracious in-laws they will try to meet the needs of the groom's family. The groom's family, who are honored guests at the wedding, will accept the decisions of the hosts with equal grace.

How many guests will there be? Once you have decided in a general way on either a large or a small wedding, calculate how many members of each family, friends, and business or professional associates, if they are to be included, you would like to invite. Figure the cost per person of the kind of wedding you have in mind, and the number of people that can be accommodated comfortably at the locale you have selected. If there are too many people for the budget or for the accommodations, you may have to pare the list.

If either or both families are very large, it may be necessary to establish a cutoff point, say, no one beyond first cousins or no children under sixteen. This is arbitrary, and in some instances painful, but it makes it easier to explain why only certain family members were invited, and reduces the possibility of anyone feeling insulted. If there are cousins too numerous to count—or to invite—it might be possible to select one representative from each family unit. Even with such methods, the hosts may still find that there are certain relatives or friends who belong at the *simḥa* (joyous occasion), no matter what blueprint has been worked out, and the only solution is—invite them.

Another way to reduce too large a list is to eliminate business and professional associates. A wedding is an event of such a personal nature, one should have no qualms about inviting only close relatives and friends.

Parents ought not to lose sight of the fact that it is their children's wedding and that the couple's friends are very important. By the same token, the bride and groom should remember that it is a time of joy for the entire family: they may not even know great-aunt Sarah, but his (or her) parents feel very close to her, and the wedding would be less joyous for them if she were absent.

It is usually unrealistic to think of the guest list in terms of "half for you, half for us." Perhaps the groom has numerous aunts, uncles, and cousins, and the bride only a few. It may be that the bride or groom or a parent is prominent in civic or business affairs, or that most members of one family simply live too far away to consider making the trip. All of these factors should be taken into careful account in order to reach a wise and practical solution.

A limited budget may require having a wedding with few guests, but this need not always be so. If the couple have numerous friends and relatives, for example, it might be best to plan a simple stand-up reception rather than a six-course seated dinner. In this way, many more people who are close to the bride and groom will have the joy of attending the wedding—which is a much greater *mitzvah* than sitting down to an elaborate banquet!

In drawing up a guest list, it is helpful to bear in mind the statistics suggested by caterers: of those invited, ninety per cent generally accept the invitation. The actual attendance is somewhat less, since usually some two per cent of those who accept are later forced to withdraw.

It is customary to include the rabbi and cantor and their wives in the guest list, whether the wedding is large or small.

Write It Down

Once the size and composition of the guest list has been determined, all names and addresses should be carefully recorded.

The groom's mother gives her list to the bride's mother, making sure that the full names and addresses are given clearly, including names of children who are to be invited.

Both families will, of course, make separate lists of persons who are not being invited to the wedding, but to whom announcements of the marriage may be sent.

There are several good methods for recording the guest list, the two most common being a card file and a large alphabetized book, like an address book. If some people are being invited only to the ceremony or only to the reception, it will be necessary either to keep separate categories or to code the names in some appropriate fashion.

The names of those who are to receive announcements may be incorporated into the guest list or recorded separately.

As the wedding date draws near, the hostess will use her notebook or file cards to compile an alphabetized list of those who have accepted the invitation. If guests are to be seated at the reception, this list will help in making the seating arrangements.

Here are two sample cards from a guest list file:

Name and address	NUMBER WILL ATTEND	UNABLE TO ATTEND	ANNOUNCEMENT
Mr. and Mrs. Jeremy Stern 214 Eckert Ave. Reading, Penn. Jonathan and Joan	4	—	—

Name and address	NUMBER WILL ATTEND	UNABLE TO ATTEND	ANNOUNCEMENT
Miss Judith Snow 520 East Fourth St. New York, N.Y.	—	—	yes

Any method may be used to record the guest list; the important thing is to have a method, one that will enable the hostess to keep track of all the necessary details with ease.

The following pages deal with the conventional forms for issuing wedding invitations, according to established American etiquette. Many people follow these patterns faithfully. Others choose to be flexible, and to adapt the established forms to their own needs and tastes. Among Jews, there are certain distinctive traditions associated with the wedding invitation, and these are dealt with as well.

THE FORMAL INVITATION

A formal invitation is usually engraved. Engraving is beautiful, but it is also quite costly, and many people prefer to use a less-expensive process called thermography, which produces an effect similar to engraving. A variety of type faces is available for either process, though any of the script styles is usually considered most formal.

The invitation is printed in black ink on white or cream-colored vellum. It is on a double sheet folded vertically, and all the printing appears on the front, or facing, page. The usual size is five by seven-and-a-half inches. It is folded in half horizontally for insertion in the envelope. A smaller size, which does not require folding, is also acceptable. If the stationer provides tissues, these should be retained; a tissue is placed over the printed surface to prevent the ink from smudging, and the invitation is then inserted in the envelope.

Two envelopes are usually provided for the invitation. The inner envelope is not sealed. It is inserted so that its front faces the recipient when he opens the outer envelope.

Addressing. The envelopes are addressed neatly by hand in black ink. A return address may be written by hand on the back flap, or it may be embossed. Engraving is considered poor form.

The full name and address of the guest appears on the outer envelope:

> Mr. and Mrs. Jeremy Stern
> 214 Eckert Avenue
> Reading, Pennsylvania

On the inner envelope, the first name and the address are omitted:

> Mr. and Mrs. Stern

If children are to be included, the phrase "and family" should be avoided, both on the outer and inner envelopes. If the children are under sixteen, only the names of the parents appear on the outer envelope. The inner envelope is addressed as follows:

Mr. and Mrs. Stern
Jonathan and Joan

If the children are over sixteen, it is proper to send them separate invitations, or a group invitation:

Mr. Jonathan Stern
Miss Joan Stern
214 Eckert Avenue
Reading, Pennsylvania

The inner envelope would then read:

Mr. Stern
Miss Stern

It is customary to mail wedding invitations three to four weeks before the wedding date. All the invitations should be mailed on the same day, using first-class postage.

When sending a formal invitation to close relatives, especially if they live far away, a personal note might well be included.

The Wording of the Invitation. The conventional invitation to a formal wedding is issued in the name of the bride's parents:

Mr. and Mrs. Haskell Price
request the honour of your presence
at the marriage of their daughter
Gloria
to
Mr. Oskar Salon
on Sunday, the twentieth of February
at one o'clock
B'nai Jeshurun Synagogue
Sixteen Wilmot Place
White Plains, New York

R.S.V.P.
Twenty-two Buck Hill Road
White Plains

Note that the phrase "request the honour of your presence" is standard usage for any formal wedding. For a less formal wedding or for a wedding reception, the phrase "request the pleasure of your company" may be substituted.

Unless the street number is unwieldy, it should always be written out in full. The year need not accompany the date on an invitation, but it is mandatory on an announcement.

First names should be written in full, and nicknames should be avoided. Titles should also be written in full, though the abbreviations "Mr.," "Mrs.," and "Dr." are acceptable.

The invitation on page 31 is for the ceremony and the reception, though neither is mentioned. This form is commonly used for Jewish weddings, particularly synagogue weddings, since one assumes that unless it is otherwise indicated, a reception will follow immediately after the ceremony.

If the reception is to take place elsewhere, however, the following is added:

> *and afterwards at*
> *the Hotel Orrington*
> *White Plains*

If the ceremony is to take place with only a few people present, and will be followed by a large reception, the invitation would be to the reception:

> *Mr. and Mrs. Haskell Price*
> *request the pleasure of your company*
> *at the wedding reception of their daughter*
> *Gloria*
> *and*
> *Mr. Oskar Salon*
> *Sunday, the twentieth of February*
> *at half after two o'clock*
> *Twenty-two Buck Hill Road*
> *White Plains, New York*

The favour of a
reply is requested

In this situation, those who are being asked to the ceremony may be invited personally, or a small card may be enclosed with the reception invitation:

> *Ceremony*
> *at one o'clock*
> *B'nai Jeshurun Synagogue*
> *White Plains*

Invitation to a Small Dinner. If, following a ceremony and reception, there is to be a dinner for a small number, the following card is enclosed with the wedding invitation:

> *Mr. and Mrs. Haskell Price*
> *request the pleasure of your company*
> *at dinner following the reception*
> *Twenty-two Buck Hill Road*
> *White Plains, New York*

R.S.V.P.

If Parents Are Widowed, Separated, or Divorced. If the bride has only one parent living, the invitation is issued in the name of that parent: Mrs. Israel Farber (never Mrs. Ruth Farber) or Mr. Israel Farber.

If the bride's parents are separated, but not divorced, the invitation may be sent in the usual manner by both parents. In the case of legal separation, however, the principals may decide that the invitation should be sent in the name of one parent, the one with whom the bride lives.

If the parents are divorced, the invitation is almost always issued in the name of the parent with whom the bride lives: Mrs. Kaufman Witkin or Mr. Julian Witkin. Note that the divorced mother uses her maiden name followed by her former husband's family name. Unlike the widow, she does not use her husband's first name.

If the widowed or divorced mother has remarried, she and her husband may issue the invitation:

> *Mr. and Mrs. Peter Rubin*
> *request the honour of your presence*
> *at the marriage of Mrs. Rubin's daughter*
> *Sarah Merle Witkin . . .*

If the bride has been adopted by her stepfather, or if the relationship is a close one, the invitation might read:

> *Mr. and Mrs. Peter Rubin*
> *request the honour of your presence*
> *at the marriage of their daughter*
> *Sarah Merle Witkin . . .*

It is sometimes desirable for a remarried widow or divorcée to issue an invitation in her name alone:

Mrs. Stanley Lauton
requests the honour of your presence
at the marriage of her daughter
Tamar Farber . . .

If the father of the bride, divorced or widowed, is giving the wedding, the invitation would be in his name only: Mr. Julian Witkin.

If he has remarried, he and his wife may issue the invitation:

Mr. and Mrs. Julian Witkin
request the honour of your presence
at the marriage of Mr. Witkin's daughter
Sarah Merle Witkin . . .

Even if remarried, he may choose to issue the invitation in his name only, and this is quite acceptable.

There are instances of divorced parents who have maintained a friendly relationship, and who wish to issue a joint invitation. Suitable wording would be:

Mrs. Kaufman Witkin
Mr. Julian Witkin
request the honour of your presence
at the marriage of their daughter
Sarah Merle Witkin . . .

Orphaned Bride. If neither of the bride's parents is living, the bride's closest relative may issue the invitation:

Mr. and Mrs. Moshe Farber
request the honour of your presence
at the marriage of their sister
Miss Tamar Farber . . .

Note that when anyone other than the bride's parents issues the invitation, the bride's full name, preceded by "Miss," is used.

A bride who has no relatives may have the invitation sent in the name of close friends:

Mr. and Mrs. Mark Hodess
request the pleasure of your company
at the marriage of
Miss Tamar Farber . . .

The bride who has no relatives may prefer to send out an invitation in her own name. The same might apply to the bride who is mature and who has established herself professionally:

The honour of your presence
is requested at the marriage of
Miss Tamar Farber . . .

Sometimes the bride is known by a professional name, and this name may be used, in parentheses, on the invitation:

Miss Tamar Farber
(Tammy Farr)

If the bride has the title of "doctor," it is not used on an invitation issued by her parents. However, if the invitation is sent out by relatives or friends or by the bride herself, she may use "Dr." before her name instead of "Miss."

Invitation from the Groom's Parents. It is unusual for the groom's parents to be hosts at a wedding, but it does occasionally happen:

Mr. and Mrs. Louis Gelber
request the honour of your presence
at the marriage of
Miss Constance Rosenman
to their son
Mr. Jonathan Gelber . . .

Divorced or Widowed Bride. If a young woman is to be married for the second time, it is customary for her parents to issue the invitation. For a young divorcée, the invitation would read:

Mr. and Mrs. Zalman Stein
request the honour of your presence
at the marriage of their daughter
Sylvia Stein Fain . . .

If she is a widow, the daughter is referred to as "Sylvia Fain," or "Sylvia Eve Fain." She generally does not use her maiden name.

The title "Mrs." is used only by a bride, usually mature, who is sending out an invitation in her own name and that of her husband-to-be. For a widow, the proper form would be:

> *The honour of your presence is*
> *requested at the marriage of*
> **Mrs. Benjamin Fain**
> *to*
> *Dr. Ethan Beck* . . .

According to formal usage, the divorcée issuing her own invitation would refer to herself as "Mrs. Stein Fain." Though the strictest usage prohibits inclusion of her first name, she may prefer to call herself "Mrs. Sylvia Stein Fain," or "Sylvia Stein Fain." This restores her personal identity to her, and still indicates that she has been divorced. To circumvent this problem, the older divorced woman may choose not to send out wedding invitations at all, but to invite her friends personally.

Groom in the Service. If the groom is serving in the armed forces, it is customary to indicate this on the invitation. If he is a noncommissioned officer or an enlisted man, the title "Mr." is eliminated from before his name, and his branch of service is given on the next line:

> *Mr. and Mrs. Haskell Price*
> *request the honour of your presence*
> *at the marriage of their daughter*
> **Gloria**
> *to*
> *Oskar Salon*
> *Infantry, United States Army*

His rank may be included, if desired:

> *Oskar Salon*
> *Ensign, United States Navy*

If the groom is a regular officer and his rank is captain or higher in the Army, Air Force, or Marine Corps, or senior-grade lieutenant or higher in the Navy, his title precedes his name:

> *Lieutenant-Colonel Oskar Salon*
> *United States Air Force*

Reserve officers use their titles only if they are on active duty.

Reception After Wedding Trip. A reception may be given by the bride's parents, by the groom's parents, or both, after the couple return from their wedding trip. A suitable formal invitation would be:

Mr. and Mrs. Howard Krohn
Dr. and Mrs. Leonard Marks
request the pleasure of your company
at a reception in honor of
Mr. and Mrs. Ira Marks
Sunday, the twentieth of February
at four o'clock
The Rothschild Club
400 Atherton Avenue
Brookline, Massachusetts

R.S.V.P.
Mrs. Krohn
20 Harvard Lane
Brookline

The Double Wedding. A joint invitation may be issued by two families whose daughters are to be married at a double wedding. The name of the bride who is older appears first, or they appear in alphabetical order:

Mr. and Mrs. Louis Gould
Mr. and Mrs. Gershon Klayman
request the honour of your presence
at the marriage of their daughters
Judith
to
Mr. Mordecai Rudin
and
Anne
to
Dr. Aaron Telnick
on Sunday, June tenth
at one o'clock
Temple Gates of Heaven
Thorndike Avenue
Philadelphia, Pennsylvania

The parents may choose to issue separate invitations, or the two invitations may be printed on the inside of a double sheet, facing each other.

If sisters are being married at a double wedding, the invitation would read as follows:

Mr. and Mrs. Samuel Idelson
request the pleasure of your company
at the marriage of their daughters
Shira Aviva
to
Mr. Jonah Ross
and
Gila Naomi
to
Mr. Michael Bender
Saturday, the tenth of November
Eight o'clock
4 Parkview Lane
Elkins Park, Pennsylvania

R.S.V.P.

Cards of Admission. If the bride or groom or any of the parents is prominent, there is always the possibility that uninvited persons may want to attend the wedding. This is most likely to occur if the wedding takes place in a synagogue. It may be desirable, therefore, to provide a special card of admission for invited guests. The card, enclosed with the invitation, might read:

Please present this card at
Temple Beth-El
Tuesday, July tenth

THE INFORMAL INVITATION

The invitation to an informal wedding may be extended in any of a number of ways, depending on the size of the guest list. If the guest list is small, the bride's mother may telephone or telegraph the invitation or may send a handwritten note on an informal:

Dear Mr. and Mrs. Godine,

    Our daughter Judith will be married to Simha Berk on Sunday, August 27, at two o'clock, at Temple Sinai, in Detroit. There will be a dinner afterward at our home.

    We would very much like to have you join us. Do let us know if you will come.

Cordially,
Hannah Poplack

When a large number of people are to be invited, handwritten notes may be impractical, and a printed—not engraved—

invitation would be in order. This could be on a folded card, approximately five by three-and-a-half inches in size, on ivory or cream stock. It might also be in the same form as a formal invitation, but in a reduced size. Only one envelope would be used for this informal invitation.

Mr. and Mrs. Hyman Poplack
cordially invite you to attend
(or, *request the pleasure of your company at*)
the marriage of their daughter
Judith
to
Mr. Simha Berk
Sunday, August 27, 1960
Two o'clock
Temple Sinai
Detroit

R.S.V.P.

RESPONSE TO INVITATION

The proper forms for responding to wedding invitations are found in Chapter X, "A Guide for Guests." In general, a formal invitation requires a formal response, and an informal invitation requires an informal response, both handwritten by the guest.

In recent years, the printed response card has come into use, though writers of etiquette books state unequivocally that this practice is in poor taste.

It may be that the practice was initiated by a thoughtful hostess who was looking for a solution to a common problem: the lack of responses or the lateness of responses to the wedding invitation. And so the printed response card with its stamped return envelope, an accepted practice in business, was adopted for use with the wedding invitation.

M_____
_____ will attend
_____ will not attend

The guest signs his name, and checks the appropriate space.

There is no doubt that though the response card is efficient, it presents a cold, businesslike face when it appears in conjunction with a wedding invitation. A handwritten response is always gracious and most fitting for an event of a social nature. It may well be, however, that some day the response card will win general approval, and that the personal, handwritten note will succumb to the rapid pace of our times.

ANNOUNCEMENTS

Announcements of a marriage may be sent to people who have not been invited to the wedding. They are most commonly used if the wedding is a small one, though there may be a need for them even if the wedding is large.

All the announcements are mailed after the ceremony on the day of the wedding or the following day. They should be ordered well in advance, perhaps at the same time as the invitations. As with the invitations, the stationer may be asked to send the envelopes first, so that the job of addressing can be started early. They are then stamped and put aside, ready for mailing.

The general rules governing invitations apply to announcements. An announcement is issued by the bride's parents or parent, or by a relative. If the bride has issued her own invitation to the wedding, the announcement is made jointly by the bride and her new husband.

Here is a standard form for an announcement:

Mr. and Mrs. Haskell Price
have the honour of announcing
the marriage of their daughter
Gloria
to
Mr. Oskar Salon
on Sunday, the twentieth of February
One thousand nine hundred and sixty-seven
at B'nai Jeshurun Synagogue
White Plains, New York

In place of the phrase "have the honour of announcing" it is possible to substitute the less-formal phrase "announce the marriage of their daughter." The full date, including the year, is spelled out. The city in which the wedding took place is included; the synagogue is optional.

Here is an announcement of a widow's marriage, issued by the couple:

Mrs. Israel Farber
and
Mr. Stanley Lauton
announce their marriage
on Wednesday, the twelfth of October
One thousand nine hundred and sixty-six
Reseda, California

If the announcement is being sent to numerous friends and relatives who live at a distance, it may be desirable to add a few lines in the lower right-hand corner:

At home
after the first of November
40 Palm Drive
Reseda

ANNOUNCEMENT WITH RECEPTION INVITATION ENCLOSED

On page 37 there is an invitation to a wedding reception given after the couple return from their honeymoon. Sometimes it may be preferable to send such an invitation on a small card which is enclosed with the announcement of the marriage:

Reception
in honour of
Mr. and Mrs. Oskar Salon
on Saturday, the first of March
at half after eight o'clock
Twenty-two Buck Hill Road
White Plains, New York

R.S.V.P.

In this case, since the bride's parents have announced the marriage, it is understood that they are the hosts at the reception. Their name is on the announcement, and the responses are sent to them.

THE "TRADITIONAL" JEWISH INVITATION

Though the invitation to a wedding is purely a matter of local custom, there are certain Jewish traditions associated with it.

In contrast to the accepted American view of marriage, which gives prominence to the bride's parents, the traditional Jewish view is that both sets of parents have an equal part in the establishment of the new family unit. The marriage is not only the personal experience of the bride and groom, it also represents a merger of their families. It is quite usual, therefore, for the names of both sets of parents to appear on the invitation:

Mr. and Mrs. Abraham Markowitz

Mr. and Mrs. Moritz Lissberger

request the honor of your presence

at the marriage of their children

Sesil

and

Joseph

on Tuesday, the fourteenth of September

Nineteen hundred and sixty-five

at seven o'clock

Young Israel of Forest Hills

67-85 Burns Ave. cor. Yellowstone Blvd.

Forest Hills, New York

In a modified version of this form, the names of the groom's parents appear following the groom's name, as in this formal invitation:

Mr. and Mrs. William D. Chananie

request the honour of your presence

at the marriage of their daughter

Ruth

to

Haskell

son of Mr. and Mrs. Ralph Zabitsky

Sunday, the fourth of November

nineteen hundred and fifty-six

at half after five o'clock

Young Israel Synagogue

Montreal

The names of departed parents may be included:

The honor of your presence is requested

at the marriage of

Vera Hallemann Zabelle

Daughter of Esther Miriam Hallemann and

the late Dr. George Hallemann

and

Morton Moshe Leifman

Son of Ida Hassia Leifman and

the late Harry Leifman

on the second day of Hanukah,

Sunday afternoon, December 23rd, 1962

at half after four o'clock

Temple Emanuel

Miami Beach, Florida

In the above example, note that reference is made to the fact that the wedding is taking place during Hanukah.

For a wedding announcement, the same forms may be repeated. Here, both sets of parents announce the marriage:

Mr. and Mrs. Morris Kaufman

Rabbi and Mrs. S. Gershon Levi

announce the marriage

of their children

Harriet Sybil

and

Don Simeon Levi

Sunday, October twenty-third

nineteen hundred and sixty

Berlin Chapel, Brandeis University

Waltham, Massachusetts

A quotation from the Bible, from the wedding service, or from another source can be a beautiful and fitting addition to an invitation.

Here is the facing, or front, page of an interesting invitation, showing two Biblical quotations printed in Torah script. The bride's Hebrew name is Rebekah, the groom's Hebrew name, Jacob. The quotations that were selected are: "And he took Rebekah, and she became his wife, and he loved her," and "And Rebekah loved Jacob."

The invitation itself is printed on the inside, in English on the left, in Hebrew on the right.

Rabbi and Mrs. Isaac Klein

request the honor of your presence

at the marriage of their daughter

Rivka

to

Mr. Gerald Berkowitz

son of

Mr. and Mrs. Samuel Berkowitz

on Sunday, the twentieth of June

Nineteen hundred and sixty-five

at three o'clock

Temple Emanu El

Colvin and Tacoma Avenues

Buffalo, New York

Reception immediately following ceremony

Not everyone is fortunate enough to find such apt Biblical quotations. There are any number of phrases that can be used on the front of an invitation. It is certainly appropriate to use the Hebrew words, but it is just as correct to use an English translation—or both. Here are some suggestions:

"And I will betroth thee unto me forever" (Hosea 2:19)

וארשתיך לי לעולם

"I am my beloved's, and my beloved is mine"

(Song of Songs 2:16)

דודי לי ואני לו

"The voice of joy and the voice of gladness, the voice of the bridegroom and the voice of the bride"

(from the Seven Wedding Blessings)

קול ששון וקול שמחה
קול חתן וקול כלה

Any of these quotations may be printed on the facing page of the invitation. The invitation itself would then be inside—on the right side, if only an English text is used.

The sample invitations and quotations given above are intended to demonstrate that even the use of a few Hebrew words, or an appropriate quotation, may add a meaningful and distinctive note to a Jewish invitation—and the desired formality can still be maintained.

In every large city there is at least one printer who specializes in Hebrew printing or who can provide Hebrew type to your own stationer or printer. Such fine stores as Tiffany's, in New York, are happy to incorporate Hebrew lettering and ask only that the customer provide a sample of the text for the engraver to work from.

Newspaper Announcements

If the bride's parents wish to announce her marriage in the newspaper, the information should be sent to the society editor well in advance of the wedding date. It is important to give a release date at the top of the notice: "Not to be released before————" (give the next date after the date of the wedding).

The wedding notice should, of course, be typed neatly, double-spaced.

In large cities, newspapers may choose to announce only the marriages of well-known people, or to print only a short announcement, or not to print the announcement at all. In small cities or towns, on the other hand, the newspapers may be happy to include descriptions of the gowns and flowers, the names of the attendants and out-of-town or prominent guests, and other details.

Prominent people should make certain to send all information in detail. Otherwise, the newspaper, eager to print a full story, may include misinformation.

The name, address, and telephone number of the bride's mother or other close relative should appear on the notice, so that the society editor can call them for additional information, or to verify the facts.

Sample News Release

Contact:	Mrs. Robert Schein	Not to be
	10 Dolbeau Place	released before
	Ridgefield, Michigan	April 27, 1967
	OL 3-4298	

Miss Phyllis Schein, daughter of Mr. and Mrs. Robert Schein, of this city, was married to Mr. Alan Waldman, son of Mr. and Mrs. Howard Waldman, of Ottawa, Ontario, on Wednesday April 26th, at the Shaarei Zion Temple. Rabbi David Moss and Cantor Benjamin Berman officiated.

Miss Abigail Schein, sister of the bride, was maid of honor. Mr. Harold Levy, a cousin of the groom, served as best man.

Mrs. Waldman is a member of the senior class at the University of Michigan. Her husband, who graduated with the class of 1965 from the same university, is now a graduate student at Columbia University.

If either set of parents is divorced, or if a parent is deceased, the wording of the announcement must be altered accordingly. See pages 8 and 9 for information regarding the correct forms to be used.

A glossy print of the bridal portrait may accompany the release, or the photographer may be asked to send it separately. It

should be understood that the newspaper will use the photo only
if space permits.

ACKNOWLEDGING WEDDING GIFTS

The bride begins to acknowledge gifts as soon as they start
arriving, in the order in which they are received. People understand that a busy bride may not be able to write immediately, but
if they do not hear from her in a month or two, they may fear
that the gift has gone astray.

The bride would be wise to arm herself with a special notebook in which to record her gifts. If she keeps it in a handy
place, it is a simple matter to jot down the necessary information
as soon as a gift is opened. There is not much point in keeping an
alphabetized list, since the important thing is to have a chrono-
logical record of the gifts, as they are received. The notebook
could be set up this way:

Name of sender	Gift	Shop	Date received	Date acknowledged
Mr. and Mrs. Harry Klein 14 Maple Street Evanston, Illinois	white damask cloth & napkins	Marshall Field	5/20	6/1

The Thank-You Note. A handwritten note is the only
gracious way to acknowledge a gift. It should be written on fine
writing paper or on informals with the bride's name. If the bride
is writing before the wedding takes place, she signs her maiden
name—"Phyllis Schein"; after the wedding day, she signs herself
"Phyllis Waldman," or "Phyllis Schein Waldman" for easier
identification.

The style of the acknowledgment is a matter of individual
taste. If the bride is doing her job properly, though, she will refer
to the actual gift, and not just thank the giver for "your beautiful
gift."

Printed Cards. There may be situations in which the bride
will not be able to acknowledge her gifts for some time. In this
case, a printed card may be sent as a preliminary acknowledgment, but it must be followed by the bride's personal note:

> Mrs. Bernard Rosen
> wishes to acknowledge receipt
> of your wedding gift, and to let
> you know that she will write to you
> personally at an early date.

A printed thank-you card with space for insertion of a picture of the bridal pair has been introduced in recent years. It is undoubtedly a novel idea, and an expensive one, but neither the novelty nor the expense alters the basic objection to the use of a printed form. If the bride wants to send wedding pictures to close friends and relatives, there is no reason why she should not enclose a picture with each personal note she writes.

Acknowledging the Office Gift. If the individual names are listed on the card accompanying the gift, it is usually best to send a note to each person. If there are too many names, or if it is a small office, there could be no possible objection to the bride writing one note addressed to "the staff," or "to my friends and colleagues." She might request that the note be posted in a central place.

Acknowledging Telegrams. The person who has sent a telegram to a wedding will be happy to learn that it was received—and appreciated. Though the bride is very busy acknowledging gifts, and taking care of numerous other matters, she ought to send a brief note, perhaps only a line or two, to those who sent telegrams. Perhaps the groom can be drafted for this task. He might write simply:

> Your telegram made us very happy.
> Many thanks.
> > Sincerely,
> > Ellen and Leonard

The parents of the couple will wish to acknowledge those telegrams that were addressed to them personally.

קוֹל חָתָן וְקוֹל כַּלָּה

IV
The
Wedding
Party

LET THE BRIDEGROOM GO FORTH FROM HIS CHAMBER
AND THE BRIDE OUT OF HER PAVILION———JOEL 2:16
יצא חתן מחדרו וכלה מחפתה

The first wedding is described in the Book of Genesis: "And the Lord God fashioned into a woman the rib that He had taken from the man, and He brought her to the man." This is said to be the basis for the practice of having wedding attendants. The sages of the Talmud interpreted the words "and brought her unto the man" to mean that God served as attendant at the marriage of Adam and Eve, and consequently, that it is a *mitzvah*, a sacred deed, to attend a bride and groom and to join in their rejoicing.

At Jewish weddings in the past, the bride and groom were usually escorted to the canopy by their parents. This was a beautiful custom, one that expressed much warmth, and many Jews still follow it. It should be made clear, however, that who escorts the bride and groom is not a matter of religious law, but of custom, and for this reason most rabbis are amenable to the wishes of those involved. At present, most Orthodox and many Conservative Jews follow the traditional pattern. Reform and some Conservative Jews have adopted general American practice, in which the bride is escorted by her father only, and her mother and the groom's parents are seated before the start of the ceremony.

And now to the wedding participants.

MAID AND MATRON OF HONOR

The bride needs at least one honor attendant, and she may have both a maid and a matron of honor, or two maids of honor. She usually selects a sister or sister-in-law, a very close friend, or a sister of the groom as her chief attendant, inviting her to serve in this capacity enough in advance to allow for the necessary preparation. Sometimes, at a very small wedding, the bride's mother performs the functions of a matron of honor.

In addition to looking beautiful, the maid of honor has the very practical job of assisting the bride through the various stages of the ceremony, so that it will proceed smoothly and gracefully. Standing to the right of and slightly behind the bride, facing the rabbi, she lifts the bride's veil to enable her to drink the first cup of wine, and then replaces it. During the ring ceremony, she holds the bride's bouquet, and if it is a double-ring ceremony, she carries the ring for the groom, handing it to the bride at the appropriate time. After the bride receives the *ketubah* (marriage contract), the maid of honor takes it and holds it until after the ceremony. She lifts the veil for the bride to drink the second cup of wine, then arranges it so that it no longer covers the bride's face, unless the rabbi indicates otherwise. If the bride is wearing a train or flowing veil, the maid of honor helps arrange it for the recessional. To accomplish this, she hands her own bouquet to the bride's mother or places it on the table.

If there are two maids of honor, they share the duties, and one stands slightly behind the other. Midway through the ceremony, after the ring is given, they change places unobtrusively, and the second maid of honor takes over.

Apart from her important role at the ceremony, the maid of honor can be extremely helpful to the bride in a number of ways. She may help with addressing invitations, checking lists, making phone calls, and so forth; help the bride dress for the wedding—and know where to lay hands on needle, thread, pins, comb, tissues, and other emergency items; see to it that bridesmaids come early to the wedding and are properly attired; assist the bride with packing for the wedding trip and lay out her going-away outfit; help the bride change after the wedding reception, then see to it that the bridal outfit is returned to the bride's home or whatever its destination may be.

BRIDESMAIDS

It is customary to have bridesmaids at any reasonably large and formal wedding, and the usual number is between two and eight. The bride chooses these attendants from among her close friends and relatives and, possibly, sisters of the groom. A bridesmaid's function is largely decorative; she is expected to look as graceful and pretty as possible. Once having accepted the invitation to be a bridesmaid, she is expected to cooperate fully with all the plans, including the selection of the outfit, to appear promptly for the rehearsal, and to offer to help the bride and her mother with whatever may be needed.

JUNIOR ATTENDANTS

A junior bridesmaid may be part of a large wedding party. She is usually between the ages of eight and fourteen. A pair of junior bridesmaids, or even a group, can present a most charming picture.

Younger children in the family, under the age of eight, may be asked to serve as flower girl, ring bearer, or page. The inclusion of these younger attendants is much less popular now than it once was, probably because it is at times difficult to rely on them to follow instructions, and they may create a distraction. If they are used, though, have them leave the procession just before reaching the canopy, and take seats in the front row in the charge of a parent or other relative. If the bride wishes, they may join the recessional.

A flower girl may strew rose petals along the path of the procession before the bride or, she may simply walk down the aisle holding a pretty nosegay or flower basket. The ring bearer carries a satin pillow to which a ring has been lightly tied or sewn. To avoid mishap, the real ring is generally not used. Using a substitute ring also makes it possible for the young fellow to leave the procession and be seated, so that he will not have to stand throughout the ceremony.

BEST MAN

The role of best man is extremely important, as well as a great honor. The groom will usually select his brother or another close relative, or his best friend. He may also choose a brother of the bride or his own father.

During the ceremony, the best man stands to the left of and slightly behind the groom, facing the rabbi. He has the wedding ring with him, readily accessible, and he hands it to the groom when asked to do so by the rabbi.

Before and after the ceremony, the best man serves as secretary, valet, and factotum, doing everything he can to assist the groom. His usual duties include coming promptly to the wedding rehearsal and helping where needed to organize the participants; at the rehearsal, advising the ushers to come early to the wedding, to be properly attired, and to know their duties; seeing to it that the groom brings the wedding ring and the marriage license to the ceremony; if asked to, serving as witness to the signing of the marriage contract; helping the groom dress (it is a good idea to provide extra collar buttons, studs, and other possible necessities, which often go astray); helping the groom pack and seeing to it that the bride's and groom's suitcases are placed in their car, ready for departure.

If the bridal couple will be going to a local hotel, the best man checks in for them and sees to it that their bags are put in their room. He also gets the fees for the rabbi and cantor from the groom, in envelopes, and presents them privately after the ceremony. In addition, the best man proposes the first toast at the reception, and, if the groom wishes, reads telegrams aloud. He contributes what he can to the sociability of the occasion. If both he and the maid of honor are single, he serves as her escort throughout the reception.

USHERS

The groom selects the ushers usually from among his close friends and relatives, and may include a brother or brothers of the bride. A good rule of thumb is to choose one usher for every fifty guests, since the ushers not only grace the procession, but are charged with the responsibility of greeting the guests and seating them.

Ushers arrive at the scene of the wedding at a stipulated time, usually an hour before the time indicated on the invitation. If possible, one or two ushers who know most of the guests and their relationships to the bride and groom can be asked to serve as head ushers. They greet the guests and assign an usher to show them to appropriate seats. At large weddings, it is customary to seat guests of the bride on the right side of the synagogue or hall and guests of the groom on the left. At Reform weddings, however, this may be reversed.

Ushers have an important role, especially at large weddings, and they must discharge it in a dignified manner, with a minimum of fuss and conversation. A list of pointers for the ushers, given to them well beforehand, will make their task easier. Such a list might include any or all of the following:

1. Seat close relatives of the bridal pair, unaccompanied older guests, and others who merit special attention in the pews or seats closest to the canopy. Arrangements should be made beforehand to keep sufficient places empty.

2. Keep the last rows free for latecomers.

3. Suggest aisle seats near the rear for guests with young children, so that they may leave unobtrusively if the children become restless.

4. If a woman enters alone, offer her your arm when escorting her to a seat.

5. Advise the guest who may appear carrying a camera or a package that it should be left in the coat room.

6. At some Orthodox weddings, men and women are seated separately, and it may be necessary to explain this to guests who are not familiar with the practice.

7. Distribute skullcaps to male guests if men are expected to cover their heads, and lace caps, provided by the hosts, to women, if head coverings are required.

8. At a synagogue wedding, ask female guests who may be wearing strapless or décolleté gowns to keep stoles or coats on for the ceremony. This should be done tactfully, of course.

If the reception is to be held at a different place from that of the ceremony, ushers may supervise the travel arrangements for the bridal party.

Even if it is decided not to have ushers as part of the processional, it is still desirable to have them help welcome and seat the guests. At a small home wedding, it is extremely helpful to have one or two men serving as ushers, directing traffic, showing people to the coat room, powder room, and so forth.

General Notes Concerning Attendants

It is an honor to be asked to serve as an attendant at the wedding of someone near and dear, but since attendants pay for their own outfits, it is not an affront to graciously decline the invitation. This is more of a problem for women, since men can rent dress clothes for a reasonable fee. Of course, the thoughtful bride will not embarrass a friend who cannot afford the outfit by inviting her, nor will she select an outfit that is beyond the means of her friends. In rare instances, the bride may offer to pay for all the attendants' outfits.

Bridal attendants may be single or married, and their spouses do not have to be asked to be part of the bridal party. At the reception, however, it is a good idea to seat husbands and wives together.

Non-Jews may serve as attendants at Conservative and Reform weddings, though generally not at Orthodox weddings.

Attendants who come to the wedding from out of town pay for their own transportation. The bride and groom provide housing for them at their own homes, in hotels, or with friends.

GIFTS TO THE ATTENDANTS

The bride and groom generally give gifts to their attendants as mementos of the occasion. If feasible, the gifts may be engraved with the wedding date and the names or intials of the bridal pair. Identical gifts are given to all the bridesmaids, and identical gifts to the ushers. For the maid of honor and the best man, the gifts should be similar to those given to bridesmaids and ushers, but more substantial.

For bridesmaids, a suitable gift might be a small piece of jewelry (bracelet, brooch, pearl drop, beads, earrings, hair clip, charm for bracelet), a very small silver tray, a compact, jewelry case, or wallet, or a fine book. For the maid or matron of honor, any of the above may be considered. For a matron of honor, already mistress of her own home, a small ceremonial object, such as a silver *mezuzah*, traveling candlesticks, or a *hallah* cover, would be fitting.

For the best man and the ushers, the gift could be cuff links, a silver belt buckle, a tie clasp, key chain, jewelry case, desk set, cigarette lighter for desk or pocket, wallet, or a fine book. If the best man is married, a ceremonial object for his home could be selected.

The younger attendants will want to be remembered too. For the flower girl, ring bearer, or page, a small piece of jewelry or a book might be chosen.

ATTENDANTS' GIFTS TO THE COUPLE

Ushers and bridesmaids may give individual wedding presents, but frequently group gifts are decided upon. If the latter, the gift may be a piece of occasional furniture, an appliance, or some other item for the home. Bridesmaids, in addition, usually give smaller gifts at whatever showers may be held in the bride's honor.

CLOTHES FOR THE WEDDING PARTY

A beautiful wedding means, among other things, beautifully gowned women, and this calls for imagination and taste. The latter is perhaps the most important ingredient, for no matter how stylish or costly, the clothes must, above all, be appropriate for the occasion. Is the wedding formal or informal, held during the day or at night, and where is it taking place? These and other factors must be taken into account, and a great deal of thought given to the styles and colors of the dresses for the wedding party. It does not matter whether the clothes come from a Paris couturier or the local Fashion Mart; the wrong dress at the wrong time, no matter how costly, can spoil the whole effect of the wedding.

THE BRIDE

A bride should strive to look modest as well as beautiful, and chooses her gown accordingly. Long or short, with or without a train, traditional or up-to-the-minute, it must be sufficiently decorous for the ceremony. At Orthodox weddings, brides wear dresses with long sleeves or long gloves with short-sleeved dresses.

For a formal wedding, daytime or evening, a full-length gown is appropriate. For an evening wedding, the gown may be more elaborate, with a longer train and fashioned of richer fabric and trimming. Generally, the presence of a train makes a gown more formal.

For an informal wedding, daytime or evening, a simply styled full-length gown or a shorter dress is appropriate. At a daytime wedding the gown may be in a pastel shade.

For a very small wedding, or if the bride does not wish to wear a bridal gown, appropriate dress would be a simple dress or suit in white or a light color. A small matching hat with veil, or veil alone, completes the costume. In the evening, the bride could wear a dress in a somewhat dressier style, also in a soft shade. She may, if she wishes, wear a corsage, or carry a Bible, perhaps adorned with a spray of flowers.

A bride usually wears her engagement ring. A string of pearls and small earrings are appropriate jewelry, but anything more would be excessive.

Make-up should always be light. This adds to the proper bridal look and, as the photographer will tell you, is likely to produce the best results in his pictures.

Gloves are optional, and it is primarily a matter of how they look with the bridal gown. If the bride does wear them, it is important that they slip off easily for the receiving of the ring.

The Bridal Veil. The Orthodox and Conservative bride always has her face veiled for the ceremony, thereby linking herself with generations of her forebears, back to Bible times. In Genesis we read that Abraham sent a trusted servant to find a wife for his son, Isaac. Eliezer, the servant, persuaded the lovely Rebekah to marry his master's son and brought her to Canaan. When they approached Abraham's tents, Isaac came out to meet her, and "she took her veil and covered herself." From that day on, the veil has been the symbol of bridal modesty.

The face veil is usually short, about a yard square, and is attached as a layer over the regular veil, which may be of any length. The face veil may be either pinned or basted to the headdress, or may be fastened with invisible hairpins so that the maid of honor can remove it easily after the bride has sipped from the second cup of wine. Most often, though, the veil is arranged so that it need not be removed, but is simply thrown back over the bride's head, leaving her face uncovered. If the bride is wearing just a small hat or cap, it is a simple matter to attach a face veil.

Sometimes the entire veil is made so that it can be removed after the ceremony, leaving just the cap or headdress. This adds to the bride's comfort during the reception. She is also more accessible to those well-wishers who cannot resist planting a kiss on her cheek.

When choosing the veil, it is best to avoid one that is too billowy and that may obstruct the profile for the bridal portrait. Smaller girls, particularly, must be careful not to get lost in too overwhelming a veil.

A beautiful moment in the Jewish wedding is the Veiling of the Bride ceremony, which takes place before the actual wedding ceremony. This is described in detail in Chapter VIII.

The Mature Bride. The woman marrying for the first time after thirty-five will be as lovely a bride as a young girl, but the style of her wedding, including dress, should be appropriate to her years. Sometimes a bride nearing forty is able to wear a full-fledged bridal gown and veil magnificently, and if this is what she has always dreamed of, she should not hesitate for a minute. But more often, the older bride will be happier in a simple gown or a suitable cocktail dress or suit. She may wear white or any of the pastels, and will add a veil or hat with veil, according to the style of her outfit.

Second Marriage. The woman marrying for the second time, whether a widow or a divorcée, generally does not wear a real bridal gown or veil. She will probably not wear white, and in general, the style of her outfit will be simple rather than elaborate. Although she does not wear a veil, a small hat or flower arrangement is appropriate, perhaps with a nose veil.

MOTHERS OF THE BRIDE AND GROOM

Since the mothers are often members of the bridal party at a Jewish wedding, their clothes should blend in with the total picture. They usually select dresses of the same length and type, but they ought never to look alike. If the bride is wearing a long gown, the mothers may wear either short or long dresses, depending on the formality of the event. What time of day the wedding is held is an important consideration, too. At a formal evening wedding, the gowns may be extremely lavish. At a daytime wedding—before five o'clock—anything that looks like evening wear is out of place. A long gown may be worn, but it should be in a more conservative style. Soft suits or ensembles in silk or other fine fabrics are most appropriate.

The mothers may choose to wear the same color, but it is usually more interesting if they select tones that harmonize or complement each other. Hats and gloves are definitely part of their costumes. White or cream-colored kid gloves are always acceptable. Gloves, by the way, should be either on or off, and should never be worn with the fingers tucked under. Handbags may be needed during the reception, but should not be carried when mothers accompany the bride and groom to the *ḥuppah*.

Corsages are optional, since quite often the gowns don't lend themselves to this adornment. It has become fashionable in some areas for the mothers to carry sheaves of roses or other long-stemmed flowers. This not only is beautiful, but adds distinction to the role of the mothers.

BRIDESMAIDS AND MAID OF HONOR

Bridesmaids wear identically styled dresses, generally in the same color. The style of their dresses should harmonize with that of the bridal gown, but the gowns need not always be floor-length. The gowns of the maid and matron of honor are either the same as those of the bridesmaids, in slightly different colors, or have minor variations in style. Usually, different bouquets are used to distinguish the honor attendants from the bridesmaids. Headdresses and slippers or shoes are identical for all bridesmaids, and the girls should agree in advance about the amount and general type of jewelry to be worn. Their make-up is never heavy.

Junior Attendants

The junior bridesmaid wears a dress similar to those of the bridesmaids, but it is generally more youthful in style.

The flower girl wears a long or short party dress or a very simple version of the junior bridesmaid's dress. She wears gloves and slippers to match. She generally wears a circlet of flowers on her head, and carries a basket of rose petals or a miniature nosegay.

The ring bearer or page wears a gray flannel or dark suit with short trousers, white shirt, navy tie, and black socks and shoes. In summer he wears a white suit, white shirt, tie, socks and shoes. A skullcap is worn if the other men in the bridal party wear them.

Some General Pointers on Clothes

Wedding dresses, particularly that of the bride, should be comfortable. What looks stunning in a magazine or on a mannequin may prove to be awkward to wear, and this can certainly detract from one's self-confidence.

If the bridal gown has a train, one or more dress rehearsals with it are essential, particularly if the bride will have to go up and down stairs.

The colors selected for the attendants and the mothers should be neither too dark nor too bright. Too many different colors may be distracting, and the use of one color alone could be monotonous, though it is currently fashionable in some areas to dress the entire bridal party in white. If you do decide on one color—other than white—you can add interest by varying it in shade and tone.

If you select dresses that are low-cut or strapless, arrange suitable covering for the period of the ceremony. A matching stole, a long or short jacket, or a large bertha collar can be a tasteful addition to a gown and may be easily removed for the reception.

Hats. Although Jewish women usually cover their heads for regular synagogue services, they seem to prefer going hatless to weddings. Jewish tradition provides no clear-cut guidance on this matter, and whether the wedding takes place in a synagogue or elsewhere has little bearing. Even the most traditional are divided: some Orthodox rabbis insist that all women wear hats; others require only the women who stand under the *ḥuppah* to cover their heads.

If the officiating rabbi or the synagogue has no policy regarding hats, it may be considered a matter of individual choice. It would seem, though, that covering one's head for a religious ceremony, especially if it takes place in a synagogue, is always correct, and thus the wisest course to follow.

GROOM, MALE ATTENDANTS, AND FATHERS

Clothes for the male members of the bridal party may not be as glamorous as those for the ladies, but they must still be chosen with taste and care. Appropriate attire for the groom, best man, ushers, and fathers is as follows:

Formal Daytime. Black or oxford gray cutaway coat, black and gray striped trousers, gray vest, white shirt with starched or pleated bosom, wing collar, black and gray ascot, black shoes and socks, gray gloves, silk hat.

Semiformal Daytime. Black or oxford gray sack coat, striped trousers, starched white shirt with turned-down collar, four-in-hand tie in black and gray stripes, black shoes and socks, gray gloves, black or gray homburg.

Sometimes the groom just will not be coerced into wearing prescribed formal or semiformal attire. If such is the case, he and the others may wear handsome black or very dark suits, as indicated for an informal daytime wedding. The wedding party will look just as attractive, and there need be no unnecessary to-do.

Informal Daytime. Black, oxford gray, or deep navy suit, white soft shirt, conservative tie, black shoes and socks, gray or black hat.

Formal Evening. Tail coat, starched white shirt, wing collar, white tie and waistcoat, patent leather or calf pumps or oxfords, black socks, silk hat, white gloves.

Semiformal Evening. Dinner jacket, starched or soft white

shirt, black bow tie, black socks, patent leather or calf evening shoes, black hat. In warm weather, a white dinner jacket is customary.

Informal Evening. Same as for informal daytime.

Daytime Garden Wedding. White or light-colored suit, four-in-hand tie in light shades, black shoes and socks, or white shoes and socks.

If the groom wishes his best man and ushers to wear identical ties and other accessories, it is customary for him to purchase them for the entire group.

If the ceremony is extremely simple with only a handful of people present, at home, or in the rabbi's study, the groom and best man will wear whatever they feel is comfortable and appropriate.

Skullcaps (Yarmulkes)

At Orthodox and Conservative weddings, male participants wear either the hats appropriate to their outfits or black or white skullcaps. The latter look most elegant in velvet. It is customary for the hosts to provide skullcaps for the men in the bridal party, and for guests. A questionable practice has grown up in recent years, namely, the providing of colored skullcaps, usually to match the color scheme of the wedding, frequently with the names of the bridal couple and the wedding date imprinted on the caps. There is no religious law prohibiting their use, but turning a religious article into a kind of party favor is considered objectionable by many people.

Kittel (White Robe)

A white robe similar to a clerical garment was the traditional wedding garb for a groom in Eastern Europe, and is still used today in some Orthodox circles. A *kittel* is associated with both solemn (Yom Kippur) and festive (the Passover Seder) occasions, and was thus considered doubly appropriate for a wedding.

THE WEDDING REHEARSAL

If the wedding is anything other than a very small, quiet affair, it is wise to include a rehearsal in the prewedding plans. This is the one way to ensure a smooth, dignified ceremony, at which every participant is sure of his role and his duties.

Set the date for the rehearsal as early as possible, and notify all members of the bridal party. The rehearsal usually takes place a few days before the wedding, but if a number of the participants are coming from out of town, it may be necessary to schedule it for the night before the event. Needless to say, a rehearsal should never be held on the Sabbath or on a holiday.

If it is absolutely impossible to hold a full-scale rehearsal, the bride and her parents should work out the plan of the processional, after carefully looking over the locale of the wedding. If there is a wedding director, he or she will serve as guide. The plan for the processional, a diagram, and other instructions should then be typed and mailed to the participants. It is then most desirable to have all attendants arrive at the wedding locale an hour or more before the ceremony, so that they can become familiar with the surroundings and perhaps hold a brief rehearsal at that time.

All the attendants, as well as the parents of the bride and groom, the wedding director, and the organist or other musicians take part in the rehearsal. Do the bride and groom rehearse too? Opinion is divided on this question. Some hold that it is as important for the bride and groom to go through their paces beforehand as it is for the attendants, so that they will feel confident about what to do. On the other hand, it is argued, even though a rehearsal is held, a wedding is not a theatrical production, and the moment when the bride and groom walk down the aisle is unique. For this reason, the bride and groom may decide to use stand-ins and be onlookers at the rehearsal. They will know what they have to do on their wedding day, and the walk down the aisle will be savored as a truly once-in-a-lifetime experience.

REHEARSAL PARTY

A small party or dinner, preferably after the rehearsal, provides a happy and intimate celebration for the bridal party. The parents of either the bride or groom, or a close friend or relative, give the party, and husbands, wives, and fiancés of the attendants are invited as well. The parents of younger attendants are included, too.

PROCESSIONAL

The procession of the bride and groom, their attendants, and their families has always been one of the most beautiful and joyous aspects of a wedding. In Eastern Europe, particularly in small towns or villages, the entire population joined in escorting the couple to the canopy, often with candlelight and rollicking musicians. In our own time, the procession tends to be more sedate, but it is still an exciting aspect of the wedding.

The number of participants in the processional depends in large measure on the size of the synagogue, chapel, or room. The *bimah*, the platform before the ark, or the part of the room where the ceremony is to take place, should not be crowded. A beautiful scene can be created with just just a few attendants, or with bridesmaids alone or ushers alone. Even at the smallest wedding, where a best man and maid of honor may be the only attendants, the processional can be most effective.

TRADITIONAL PROCESSIONAL

The rabbi and cantor may lead the processional, or they may make their way to the *huppah* from a side door, arriving there ahead of the others. Ask the rabbi which practice he follows.

PROCESSIONAL 1

Cantor   Rabbi
Bride's Grandparents
Groom's Grandparents
Usher   Usher
Usher   Usher
Best Man
Groom's Father   Groom   Groom's Mother
Bridesmaid   Bridesmaid
Bridesmaid   Bridesmaid
Maid of Honor
Bride's Father   Bride   Bride's Mother

If the couple's grandparents are included in the processional, they follow the clergy. The processional continues with the ushers, walking singly or in pairs, about six paces apart, the shorter preceding the taller. They take their places either (A) spaced along the aisle; (B) to the right and left of the *bimah*, where the bridesmaids join them; or (C) to the left of the *bimah*, leaving the right side for the bridesmaids. (See diagrams on next page.) The decision as to how the ushers and bridesmaids will be placed depends on the size and layout of the area, personal preferences of the bride and groom, and established practices of the synagogue or hall. During the ceremony, they all face the canopy.

The best man follows the ushers, after a pause of about ten paces. He proceeds to the *ḥuppah* and stands on the left at a right angle to the rabbi.

Now the groom enters, accompanied by his parents. The groom's father is on his left, and he holds his father's arm, while his mother is on his right arm. If the groom has but one parent, he is escorted by that one. If neither parent is living, an uncle and aunt, sister and brother-in-law, brother and sister-in-law, or other close relatives or friends may accompany him. At times the best man serves as the escort. When they reach the *ḥuppah*, the groom takes his place on the left side, facing the rabbi. His parents stand next to the best man, beneath the canopy if there is room, or just outside it.

After the groom reaches the *ḥuppah*, the bridesmaids (preceded by junior bridesmaids, if any) come down the aisle, singly or in pairs, generally about six paces apart. They take their places, either (A) spaced along the aisle, (B) to the right and left of the *bimah*, or (C) to the right of the *bimah*.

Following the bridesmaids by at least ten paces, comes the maid or matron of honor. She takes her place opposite the best man, on the right side of the *ḥuppah*. If there are two honor attendants, they walk together or separately, the maid of honor preceding the matron of honor. Under the canopy, one stands slightly behind and to the right of the first, and they change places unobtrusively at the designated point in the ceremony.

If there is a flower girl, she follows the maid of honor. She takes her place in the first row, since it is too much to ask her to stand throughout the ceremony. A ring bearer precedes the flower girl, and he, too, is seated in the first row.

Now the stage is set for the bride to make her way with due pomp. As the music for the bride begins, the groom turns so that he can watch his bride approach. She is escorted down the aisle by her parents; she holds her bouquet in her right hand, while her left is on her father's arm, her right arm held by her mother.

BRIDESMAIDS AND USHERS

A

BRIDESMAIDS AND USHERS

B

BRIDESMAIDS AND USHERS

C

When they reach the *ḥuppah* the bride takes her place at the groom's right, in remembrance of the verse "at thy right hand doth stand the queen" (Psalms 45:10). Her parents stand to the right of the maid of honor, beneath the canopy if there is room, or just outside it.

If the aisle is too narrow for three to walk abreast, the groom's parents walk directly in front of him, and the bride's parents in front of her. As each set of parents nears the *ḥuppah*, they pause, facing each other across the aisle, until their child has taken his place. The parents then move into their designated positions beneath or near the canopy.

Grandparents. If grandparents are to be present, they may be asked if they care to join the processional. They may enter first, before the ushers, as in the processional on p. 66, or the groom's grandparents before the ushers and the bride's grandparents before the bridesmaids. They walk down the aisle and then leave the processional to take seats when they reach the first

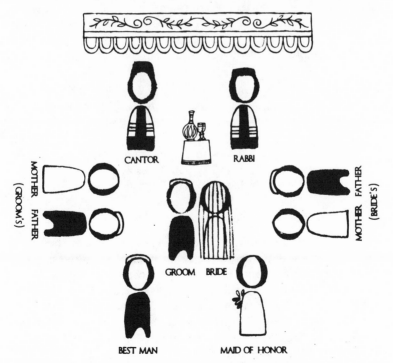

Bridal party under the canopy when traditional processional is used

row. If there is only one grandparent, he or she should be escorted down the aisle by an usher, son, or grandson. If grandparents do not walk in the processional, they may be seated at the same time as other guests in reserved places up front. If there is a Veiling of the Bride ceremony, they may remain with the bridal party until the bride has been veiled, and be escorted to their seats just before the start of the processional.

STANDARD AMERICAN PROCESSIONAL

As was mentioned at the start of this chapter, the major difference between a traditional Jewish processional and the accepted American version is that in the former the bride and groom are escorted by both parents, and in the latter, only the bride is escorted, by her father. If general American practice is followed, the groom's parents and the bride's mother are seated, before the processional begins, in the first row. The bride's mother is escorted, of course, by an usher; frequently her own son or another close relative is selected. The Jewish tradition is for the bride's family to occupy seats on the right side, and the groom's family the left, but American custom calls for the reverse.

PROCESSIONAL 2
(Rabbi, cantor, best man, and groom enter from side and stand under canopy)

Usher	Usher
Usher	Usher
Bridesmaid	Bridesmaid
Bridesmaid	Bridesmaid
Maid of Honor	
Bride's Father	Bride

The rabbi and cantor may lead the processional, or they may choose not to walk down the aisle, but to enter from the side and take their places when the music for the processional begins.

The best man and the groom usually enter from the side, following the rabbi and cantor, and take their places.

The ushers lead the processional, and are followed by the bridesmaids. See the diagrams on page 68 for the variations in placement of the ushers and bridesmaids.

The maid of honor follows the bridesmaids, and if there are a ring bearer and flower girl, they come next, in that order.

The bride enters last on her father's arm. Which arm does she take? It is probably best to resolve this in accordance with where the father is to sit. If the right side is for the bride's family, she should take her father's left arm and hold her bouquet in her left hand. If the bride's family is sitting on the left, however, she takes her father's right arm. These arrangements make it possible for the father to take his seat next to his wife with a minimum of movement.

As the bride and her father approach the canopy or the bridal table, the groom steps forward. The father places his daughter's hand in that of the groom's, and takes his seat. The groom leads the bride to her place at his side.

VARIATIONS

There is nothing sacred about the order of the processional. The two forms described above are used frequently, but variations are permitted and practiced in all Jewish groups.

Among some Orothodox Jews, for example, both fathers walk

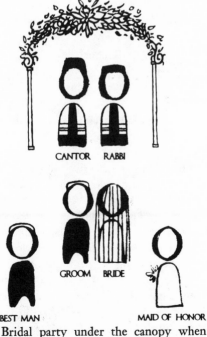

CANTOR   RABBI

GROOM   BRIDE

BEST MAN   MAID OF HONOR

Bridal party under the canopy when standard American processional is used

with the groom, and both mothers with the bride. In this situation, the fathers stand together under the *ḥuppah*, next to the groom, and the mothers stand on the right, next to the bride.

PROCESSIONAL 3

Cantor	Rabbi
Usher	Usher
Usher	Usher
Best Man	Groom
Bridesmaid	Bridesmaid
Bridesmaid	Bridesmaid
Maid of Honor	
Ring Bearer	
Flower Girl	
Bride's Father	Bride

PROCESSIONAL 4
*(Rabbi and cantor enter from
side and stand under canopy)*

Usher	Usher
Usher	Usher
Groom's Father	Groom's Mother
Best Man	
Groom	
Bridesmaid	Bridesmaid
Bridesmaid	Bridesmaid
Usher	Bride's Mother
Maid of Honor	
Bride	Bride's Father

At many Reform and Conservative weddings, the groom and the best man walk down the aisle, either together (Processional 3) or with the groom following the best man (Processional 4).

At some Conservative weddings, the processional incorporates both the traditional and the standard American forms (4). The groom's parents walk down the aisle, followed by the best man and then by the groom. The mother of the bride comes down the aisle on the arm of an usher, followed by the maid of honor, and then by the bride with her father. When this pattern is followed, the parents may either take seats in the first row, or may stand under the *ḥuppah* with their children.

THE HOME WEDDING

There are usually fewer participants in the processional at a home wedding, but the general pattern is the same as for a larger wedding. In an apartment or ranch-type house, the bridal party would enter from the front hall, or from a bedroom. In a multi-story house, the processional starts upstairs, and the group descends in designated order.

SEPARATED, DIVORCED, OR WIDOWED PARENTS

The fact that the parents of either bride or groom are separated should not be allowed to interfere with the joy of the occasion. All procedures for issuing the invitation, arranging the processional, receiving line, and so forth are followed as if the parents were living together.

The situation when parents are divorced is different. (See Chapter III regarding the issuing of the invitation.) At weddings in which the parents do not walk down the aisle or stand under the *ḥuppah*, the divorced mother is seated in the first row and her former husband in the second row. If the bride's parents are divorced, she may be escorted down the aisle by her father or, if she chooses, by another male relative. If the latter course is followed, the relative who escorts the bride to the canopy then takes a seat in the first row near the bride's mother and his own wife, if he is married.

When the traditional Jewish processional is used, it is customary for the parent with whom the child lives to be the escort. This is not always adhered to rigidly, however. For example, if the bride has her heart set on walking down the aisle on her father's arm even though she lives with her mother, her mother will surely want this wish granted. There are even situations in which both parents may escort the child, but this is rare.

The question of who is to stand under the *ḥuppah* requires delicate handling, and here, too, the wishes of the bride or groom, as the case may be, ought to be decisive. Even though the decision may be painful to either or both parents, it is *their* child's day, and his or her happiness must be the primary consideration.

It is undoubtedly easiest if the other set of parents decides not to stand under the canopy, but simply to take their seats when they reach the first row. However, if it is decided that all parents are to stand under the *huppah*, the parent who does not walk down the aisle leaves his or her seat a few seconds before the bride or groom approaches and takes his or her place under the canopy. This parent may take a seat in the first row for the recessional or may participate in it, escorted by a son or daughter, a close friend, or a relative.

A widowed parent may, of course, accompany a child to the *huppah*, but sometimes is reluctant to do so. In such a case, the parent is seated in the first row, and the child is escorted down the aisle by an uncle or brother, or, in the case of the groom, by the best man. Just before the bride or groom reaches the first row, the widowed parent rises and takes his or her place under the canopy. The parent participates in the recessional, and may be escorted by a son or daughter who has been seated in the first row.

A Very Small Wedding

Sometimes a very small wedding is held in a chapel, and the participants do not wish to walk down the aisle, even though it is shorter than the aisle in the main sanctuary. In this situation, it is best for all members of the bridal party to enter from the side, leaving only a short walk to the canopy.

The Double Wedding

A double wedding is a relatively rare occurrence, but there are times when it is necessary.

Though Jewish law permits a double wedding to take place, our tradition does not encourage the practice. The rabbis of the Talmud said that we should not allow one *simha* to diminish the importance of another. For this reason, if two children of the same parents are to be married at the same time, it is recommended that separate ceremonies be performed. In this situation, while the first marriage is being solemnized, the second couple waits their turn at the rear of the synagogue or hall. The parents who are involved in both marriages participate in both processionals, escorting first one child and then the other to the canopy. Generally, the older child is married first.

If two children of the same parents are not involved, the two couples may be married with one ceremony. There will be two ring ceremonies, of course, and the two marriage agreements (*ketubot*) will be read.

For this double wedding, the older of the two couples come to the *ḥuppah* first, with their attendants, and when they have taken their places, the second couple, with their attendants, follow:

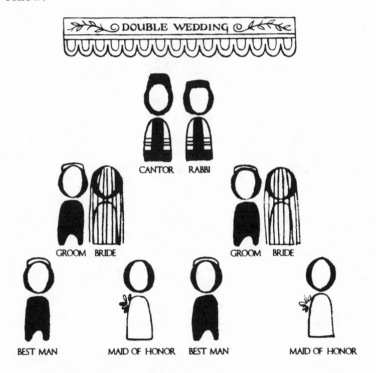

DOUBLE WEDDING

CANTOR   RABBI

GROOM BRIDE   GROOM BRIDE

BEST MAN   MAID OF HONOR   BEST MAN   MAID OF HONOR

If space allows, all the parents may choose to stand near the canopy. If this is not possible, the parents take seats in the first row after escorting their children to the canopy.

RECESSIONAL

The recessional is a joyous conclusion to the marriage ceremony, and though everyone is now more relaxed, the mood is still one of order and dignity.

The bride and groom lead the way, proceeding in an unhurried manner, to allow the guests a good look at the new and very happy pair. After the couple have walked the length of the aisle, assuming it is not too long, the other members of the bridal party follow, approximately four paces apart. They, too, walk in a measured step, in this order:

Page
Bride's Parents
Groom's Parents
Rabbi and Cantor
Grandparents
Maid of Honor with Best Man
Matron of Honor
Flower Girl
Ring Bearer
Bridesmaids
Ushers

There may be variations on this pattern, depending on the number of participants in the processional, the physical arrangement of the synagogue or hall, and personal preference. Sometimes, for example, the bridesmaids and ushers walk out in pairs; this makes a pretty picture, and calls for careful planning and rehearsing.

RECEIVING LINE

Mazal Tov! The ceremony is over, a man and a woman have been united in marriage, and now the guests must have an opportunity to greet the members of the bridal party and to extend personal good wishes. The place for the receiving line has been carefully selected beforehand to allow ample room for movement of the guests. The mother of the bride, as official hostess, has informed the participants where they will stand, and in what order. If necessary, she carries this information on a slip of paper in her bag. The participants in the receiving line take their places quickly and gracefully, as soon as the recessional is completed—unless, of course, the receiving line and reception are to be held elsewhere.

The bride's mother is first in the receiving line, and the usual order is as follows:

Bride's Mother	Bride's Father	Bride	Groom	Groom's Mother	Groom's Father

When the two families do not know each other well, the line might be better arranged as follows, so that guests can be greeted and introduced without embarrassment:

Bride's	Groom's			Groom's	Bride's
Mother	Father	Bride	Groom	Mother	Father

If the bride's mother is not living, her father will be first in line. In the event that he has remarried, his wife serves as official hostess. If neither parent is living, an aunt or other close relative of the bride may be asked to assume this position. If the bride's parents are divorced, the parent who is giving the wedding acts as host. It is not uncommon for the other parent to attend the ceremony only, and not the reception. Divorced parents of the groom, whether remarried or not, may stand in the receiving line, if this is the groom's wish.

Grandparents may be included in the receiving line—if they wish, and if they can stand the strain!

At a wedding at which *Yiḥud* is observed (see p. 134), there is no receiving line following the ceremony. Instead, bride and groom receive before the ceremony. This takes place in separate rooms, the bride surrounded by her female relatives and friends, the groom by his male relatives and friends.

V
THE
MARRIAGE CEREMONY

הרי את מקדשת לי

BEHOLD, THOU ART CONSECRATED UNTO ME. FROM THE MARRIAGE SERVICE

The high point of the Jewish wedding is the religious ceremony. The ceremony alone conveys the true meaning of marriage and underscores its sacred quality. All else, the place, the reception, the clothes, and the flowers, are merely ornaments to embellish the occasion.

ORIGINS

The ceremony, as we know it today, combines many elements, some dating back to Biblical times, most added in the course of the centuries Jews have lived in different lands. Wherever Jews settled, they adopted customs of the land and incorporated them with earlier traditions. For this reason, the marriage of an American Jewish couple is similar in many respects to that of an American Protestant or Catholic couple, while a Yemenite wedding in Israel is quite foreign to most westernized Jews, because the Yemenite Jews were influenced by the customs of the Arabs, among whom they lived for so long.

The varying customs practiced by Jews around the world would fill a huge compendium of folklore, but the core of the wedding ritual remains the same for all Jews.

At the time of the Talmud, Jewish law considered a couple legally wed if they performed any of the following three acts in the presence of at least two witnesses:

1. Presentation of an article of value to the woman.
2. Presentation of a written document to the woman.
3. Cohabitation (in this case, it was considered proper for the witnesses to remain outside the door).

Subsequent Jewish law developed more elaborate forms for consecrating marriages, but it is interesting to see that the first two of the ancient forms of marriage, and to some extent the third, are still present in most twentieth-century Jewish ceremonies.

THE RING—AN ARTICLE OF VALUE

The ring is a relatively modern substitute for the gold coin or other article of value with which a man literally purchased his wife from her father. According to custom, the ring is of plain metal and without stones, though not necessarily of pure gold. The original purpose of the requirement for plain metal was to eliminate any possible doubt in the minds of the bride and her family as to the true value of the object, particularly if gems were involved. Over the years, however, as marriage ceased to be a purchase and the ring became a symbol only, other interpretations were attached to the same requirement. For example, the solid, unbroken metal ring symbolizes the hoped-for harmony of the marriage, which should be unmarred in every way. The use of a plain band for all brides also indicates that at the sacred moment of marriage there is no difference between rich and poor.

According to Jewish law, the giving and accepting of the ring in the presence of witnesses is the most important part of the ceremony, and the marriage is in fact legalized when the groom places the ring on the bride's finger and pronounces the formula: "Behold thou art consecrated unto me with this ring, according to the law of Moses and Israel."

Because of its legal significance, the ring used at the ceremony should actually belong to the groom, and should not be borrowed for the occasion.

Ketubah — The Written Document

This is a legal contract, setting forth in writing the terms of the marriage agreement. There is no mention in the Bible of such a document, but historians have evidence proving its existence in very ancient times. There is, for example, an Egyptian papyrus *ketubah* text, which dates back to about 440 B.C.E.

Since marriage in the ancient world was a business transaction, and the woman was treated as a form of property, the earliest marriage contracts were strictly commercial agreements. However, when the Jewish marriage contract was formalized by the Sanhedrin in Jerusalem in the first century B.C.E., it was transformed into a virtual bill of rights for the wife. Because Jewish law had always permitted a man considerable leniency in divorcing his wife, the rabbis felt it desirable to protect the woman by inserting into the *ketubah* terms for the return of her dowry and other property should she be divorced or widowed. Thus, the married woman would be legally protected, and perhaps more important, her husband would be effectively discouraged from casting her aside. One-sided divorces might still occur, but the *ketubah* unquestionably served to elevate the status of woman centuries before she ever dreamed of equal rights.

In formulating the *ketubah*, the rabbis set fixed monetary terms, so that even the poorest woman was provided for. Though the monetary terms are now wholly symbolic, the Jewish bride of the twentieth century still receives a *ketubah* indicating that she has brought with her a dowry of one hundred silver pieces, that the groom has added one hundred silver pieces of his own, and that the total amount will be set aside for her protection.

The *ketubah* is written in Aramaic, which was the spoken language of the Jews during the Second Commonwealth. In addition to the monetary terms of the agreement, the bridegroom pledges to the bride to "work for thee, honor and support and maintain thee in accordance with the customs of Jewish husbands who work for their wives and who honor, support, and maintain them in truth."

The *ketubah* is signed by the two witnesses before the ceremony. The modern *ketubah* frequently makes provision for the signatures of the bride and groom, though these signatures are not essential to the legality of the document. It is the custom of most rabbis to read the *ketubah* aloud during the ceremony, in the original and in translation, in whole or in part. The *ketubah* is then given to the bride by the groom, and she retains it as her personal possession from that day onward.

The ring and the *ketubah* are the oldest features of Jewish marriage and still the most important. They have now become part of a larger ceremony which is itself a beautiful blending of stirring words and rituals.

Huppah — The Marriage Canopy

Conservative, Orthodox, and many Reform ceremonies are conducted under a *huppah*, a marriage canopy. The canopy is a faint echo of the Jews' tribal heritage, perhaps symbolic of the third legal form of marriage, cohabitation. In earliest times, the bride was led to the groom's tent or chamber, where the marriage was consummated. The Biblical word for this tent is *huppah*, which literally means "a covering."

Conditions changed in the years and centuries of Jewish

dispersion. In their crowded villages and ghettos, few young men owned a home or even a room, and frequently the bride's family had to house the couple. So the original practice faded from use, and in its place, by a slow process, of course, emerged the canopy under which the wedding blessings were recited.

An early version of the canopy was the *tallit*, the prayer shawl worn by Jewish men, which was spread above the heads of the couple. In Israel today, the *tallit* is still used for this purpose. Sephardic Jews throughout the world make use of both customs; the couple stand under a canopy, and a *tallit* covers their heads.

In this country, the *ḥuppah* is usually a silk or velvet cloth with gold fringes and embroidery, supported on four poles. It is frequently decorated with leaves and fresh flowers, particularly at formal weddings. In recent years, canopies made entirely of flowers have become common. No matter what the actual appearance of the *ḥuppah*, it is now considered a symbol of the new home which will be created by the bride and groom.

ORDER OF THE CEREMONY

The Jewish ceremony combines the betrothal (*eirusin*) and the marriage itself (*nisu 'in*). In earlier times, marriage generally took place a year after the formal betrothal, though the latter was considered as binding legally as the marriage, and could be dissolved only by divorce. By the Middle Ages, however, the custom of a year-long betrothal had almost disappeared, and since then the two ceremonies have been performed together.

INVOCATION

Blessed may you be who come in the name of the Lord; we bless you out of the house of the Lord. May He who is mighty, blessed and great above all, may He send His abounding blessings to the bridegroom and the bride.

THE BETROTHAL BENEDICTION
(*Recited Over a Cup of Wine*)

Blessed art Thou, O Lord our God, King of the universe, who createst the fruit of the vine, symbol of joy. Blessed art Thou, O Lord our God, King of the universe, who has hallowed us by Thy commandments, and has commanded us concerning forbidden marriages; who has disallowed unto us those that are betrothed, but has sanctioned unto us such as are wedded to us by the rite of the nuptial canopy and the sacred covenant of marriage. Blessed art Thou, O Lord, who hallowest Thy people, Israel, by the rite of the nuptial canopy and the sacred covenant of marriage.

(Bride and groom drink from the first cup of wine.)

RING CEREMONY

(The bridegroom places the ring on the forefinger of the bride's right hand, and recites:)

הרי את מקדשת לי בטבעת זו כדת משה וישראל

Harei at mekudeshet li betaba'at zo kedat Moshe v'yisra'el.

Thou art consecrated unto me with this ring as my wife, according to the law of Moses and Israel.

READING OF THE KETUBAH:
THE SEVEN BENEDICTIONS (SHEVA
BERAKHOT)
(*Recited Over Second Cup of Wine*)

Blessed art Thou, O Lord our God, King of the universe, who createst the fruit of the vine, symbol of joy.

Blessed art Thou, O Lord our God, King of the universe, who has created all things to Thy glory.

Blessed art Thou, O Lord our God, King of the universe, Creator of man.

Blessed art Thou, O Lord our God, King of the universe, who has made man in Thine image after Thy likeness, and has fashioned woman from man as his mate, that together they may perpetuate life. Blessed art Thou, O Lord, Creator of man.

May Zion rejoice as her children are restored to her in joy. Blessed art Thou, O Lord, who causes Zion to rejoice at her children's return.

O make these loved companions greatly to rejoice, even as of old Thou didst gladden Thy creatures in the Garden of Eden. Blessed art Thou, O Lord, who makest bridegroom and bride to rejoice.

Blessed art Thou, O Lord our God, King of the universe, who has created joy and gladness, bridegroom and bride, mirth and exultation, pleasure and delight, love, brotherhood, peace and fellowship. Soon may there be heard in the cities of Judah, and

in the streets of Jerusalem, the voice of joy and gladness, the voice
of the bridegroom and the voice of the bride, the jubilant voices
of those joined in marriage under the bridal canopy, and of youths
feasting and singing. Blessed art Thou, O Lord, who makest the
bridegroom to rejoice with the bride.

(Bride and groom drink from second cup of wine.)

BREAKING OF THE GLASS

At the conclusion of the ceremony, at most weddings, the
bridegroom breaks a glass by stepping on it. This act is intended
to temper the joy of the occasion by reminding those present of
the destruction of the Temples in Jerusalem and of other calami-
ties that befell the Jewish people. It is not, as some people think,
a sign of good luck.

This custom dates back at least to Talmudic times. The
Talmud relates a story of one of the sages who arranged a marriage feast for his son. "He observed that the rabbis present were
very gay. So he seized a costly goblet worth four hundred zuzim
and broke it before them. Thus he made them somber."

At Sephardic Jewish weddings, the following verses from
Psalm 137 are recited when the glass is broken: "If I forget thee,
O Jerusalem, let my right hand forget her cunning. Let my
tongue cleave to the roof of my mouth, if I remember thee not;
if I set not Jerusalem above my chiefest joy."

THE BENEDICTION

Today many marriage ceremonies are concluded with the
priestly benediction, pronounced by the rabbi:

May the Lord bless you and protect you,
May the Lord show you favor and be gracious to you,
May the Lord turn in loving kindness to you and grant you peace.
                                                              Amen.

SOME VARIATIONS IN
WEDDING PRACTICE

The marriage ceremony and the rituals described above reflect
traditional Jewish practice. However, variations are to be found

in present-day American Judaism, and within each of the three groups one can find differing views and practices. Some of the most accepted practices are described below, but in every instance the bride and groom should discuss each point with the officiating rabbi or with an official of the synagogue in which the wedding is to take place.

THE RING

The requirement that the wedding band be of plain metal is maintained by most Orthodox and by many Conservative rabbis, though an engraved ring is often permitted.

A double-ring ceremony is frequently performed at Conservative and Reform ceremonies, and occasionally at Orthodox weddings. Orthodox rabbis generally prefer that the bride give the ring to the groom after the service takes place.

The groom receives his ring after he has recited the blessing and has placed the ring on the finger of the bride; she, in turn, slips his ring on the ring finger of his left hand. She need not recite anything, but many rabbis use a special declaration for the bride to recite as well.

There is a new look in wedding rings created in recent years by a group of Jewish craftsmen. Some rings are worked with quotations from the Song of Songs. In others, the Hebrew names of the bride and groom are interwoven in raised letters. These rings are available in many jewelry shops in New York City or in stores selling ceremonial objects.

THE KETUBAH

The *ketubah* is required at all Orthodox and Conservative marriages. In Reform Judaism, a Certificate of Marriage, signed by the rabbi and two witnesses, is presented to the couple but not read at the ceremony.

Conservative rabbis may use a *ketubah* that contains an addition to the traditional text. The new clause states that if the marriage is ever dissolved under civil law, either party may invoke the authority of the Conservative rabbinical court to determine "what action by either spouse is then appropriate under Jewish matrimonial law; and if either spouse shall fail to honor the demand of the other or to carry out the decision of the

בס"ד

This Is To Certify

That on the____day of the week, the____day of the month_____in the year 57____ corresponding to the____day of_____ 19____, the holy Covenant of Marriage was entered into, in_____between the Bridegroom_____ and his Bride_____

The said Bridegroom made the following declaration to his Bride: "Be thou my wife according to the law of Moses and of Israel. I faithfully promise that I will be a true husband unto thee. I will honor and cherish thee; I will work for thee; I will protect and support thee, and will provide all that is necessary for thy due sustenance, even as it becomes a Jewish husband to do. I also take upon myself all such further obligations for thy maintenance as are prescribed by our religious statute."

And the said Bride has plighted her troth unto him, in affection and sincerity, and has thus taken upon herself the fulfilment of all the duties incumbent upon a Jewish wife.

This Covenant of Marriage was duly executed and witnessed this day according to the usage of Israel.

_____

_____   _____
Rabbi   **Witnesses**

בס״ד

בְּשַׁבָּת _____ לְחֹדֶשׁ _____
שְׁנַת חֲמֵשֶׁת אֲלָפִים וּשְׁבַע מֵאוֹת _____ לִבְרִיאַת עוֹלָם לְמִנְיַן
שֶׁאָנוּ מוֹנִין כָּאן _____ בִּמְדִינַת _____
אֵיךְ הֶחָתָן _____ בַּר _____
אָמַר לָהּ לַהֲדָא _____
בַּת _____ , הֲוֵי לִי לְאִנְתּוּ כְּדַת מֹשֶׁה
וְיִשְׂרָאֵל וַאֲנָא אֶפְלַח וְאוֹקִיר וְאֵיזוֹן וַאֲפַרְנַס יָתִיכִי לִיכִי כְּהִלְכוֹת גּוּבְרִין
יְהוּדָאִין דְּפָלְחִין וּמוֹקְרִין וְזָנִין וּמְפַרְנְסִין לִנְשֵׁיהוֹן בְּקֻשְׁטָא וְיָהֵבְנָא לִיכִי
מֹהַר _____ כְּסַף זוּזֵי _____ דְּחָזֵי לִיכִי _____
וּמְזוֹנַיְכִי וּכְסוּתַיְכִי וְסִפּוּקַיְכִי וּמֵיעַל לְוָתַיְכִי כְּאֹרַח כָּל אַרְעָא. וְצָבִיאַת
מָרַת _____ , דָּא הֲוַת לֵהּ לְאִנְתּוּ. וְדֵין
נְדוּנְיָא דְּהַנְעֵלַת לֵהּ מִבֵּי _____ בֵּין בְּכֶסֶף בֵּין בְּדָהָב בֵּין בְּתַכְשִׁיטִין
בְּמָאנֵי דִלְבוּשָׁא בְּשִׁמּוּשֵׁי דִירָה וּבְשִׁמּוּשֵׁי דְּעַרְסָא. הַכֹּל קִבֵּל עָלָיו _____
חָתָן דְּנָן _____ זְקוּקִים כְּסַף צָרוּף. וְצָבִי
חָתָן דְּנָן וְהוֹסִיף לָהּ מִן דִּילֵהּ עוֹד _____
_____ זְקוּקִים כְּסַף צָרוּף אֲחֵרִים כְּנֶגְדָּן, סַךְ הַכֹּל
_____ זְקוּקִים כְּסַף צָרוּף. וְכָךְ אָמַר
חָתָן דְּנָן, אַחֲרָיוּת שְׁטַר כְּתֻבְּתָא דָּא נְדוּנְיָא דֵן וְתוֹסֶפְתָּא דָא קַבְּלִית עָלַי
וְעַל יָרְתַי בַּתְרָאי לְהִתְפְּרַע מִכָּל שְׁפַר אֲרַג נִכְסִין וְקִנְיָנִין דְּאִית לִי תְּחוֹת
כָּל שְׁמַיָּא, דְּקְנָאִי וּדְעָתִיד אֲנָא לְמִקְנָא, נִכְסִין דְּאִית לְהוֹן אַחֲרָיוּת וּדְלֵית
לְהוֹן אַחֲרָיוּת כֻּלְּהוֹן יְהוֹן אַחֲרָאִין וְעַרְבָאִין לִפְרוֹעַ מִנְּהוֹן שְׁטַר כְּתֻבְּתָא
דָּא נְדוּנְיָא דֵן וְתוֹסֶפְתָּא דָא מִנַּאי וַאֲפִלּוּ מִן גְּלִימָא דְעַל כַּתְפָּאי בְּחַיַּי
וּבָתַר חַיַּי מִן יוֹמָא דְנָן וּלְעָלַם. וְאַחֲרָיוּת שְׁטַר כְּתֻבְּתָא דָא נְדוּנְיָא דֵן
וְתוֹסֶפְתָּא דָא, קִבֵּל עָלָיו _____ חָתָן דְּנָן
כְּחֹמֶר כָּל שְׁטָרֵי כְתֻבּוֹת וְתוֹסֶפְתּוֹת דְּנָהֲגִין בִּבְנוֹת יִשְׂרָאֵל הָעֲשׂוּיִין כְּתִקּוּן
חֲכָמֵינוּ זִכְרָם לִבְרָכָה דְּלָא כְאַסְמַכְתָּא וּדְלָא כְּטוֹפְסֵי דִשְׁטָרֵי. וְקָנִינָא מִן
_____ חָתָן דְּנָן לְמָרַת _____ בַּר
_____ בַּת
דָּא עַל כָּל מַה דִּכְתוּב וּמְפֹרָשׁ לְעֵיל בְּמָנָא דְּכָשֵׁר לְמִקְנָא בֵּהּ.
וְהַכֹּל שָׁרִיר וְקַיָּם.

נְאֻם _____
נְאֻם _____

Traditional *Ketubah*
(marriage contract)

Certificate of marriage issued to Reform Jewish couples

Bet Din (rabbinic court) or its representatives, then the other spouse may invoke any and all remedies available in civil law and equity to enforce compliance with the *Bet Din's* decision and this solemn obligation. . . ." This amendment was introduced primarily to protect a woman whose husband might refuse to grant her a Jewish religious divorce, and thereby prevent her from ever remarrying in a religious ceremony.

The *ketubah* itself can be a beautiful work of art. In years past, it was not uncommon for a family to commission an artist to create an illuminated *ketubah* for a particular marriage. Many examples of these can be seen in the Jewish Museum in New York, and in the Museum of the Hebrew Union College–Jewish Institute of Religion in Cincinnati. Today, a couple may still find a Jewish artist who specializes in calligraphy and illumination and commission him to execute a distinctive *ketubah*.

THE HUPPAH

Orthodox and Conservative ceremonies are always conducted under a bridal canopy. In Reform Judaism, a canopy is not mandatory, and its use is usually dependent on the wishes of the bridal pair and the consent of the rabbi.

MINYAN

According to tradition, a quorum of ten adult males (*minyan*) is required at all public religious ceremonies, including weddings. Orthodox and Conservative rabbis will generally urge the maintenance of this tradition. Even at small weddings, families are requested to provide a *minyan* for the ceremony. The ceremony is legally valid, however, as long as proper witnesses are present.

WITNESSES

Two witnesses are required at all Jewish wedding ceremonies. In Orthodox and Conservative marriages the main duties of the witnesses are to sign the *ketubah*, in Hebrew, and to witness the ring ceremony, to make certain that it is performed in the prescribed legal manner. Legal witnesses are any two adult Jewish males, not related either by blood or marriage to the bride or groom, and who are religiously observant. It is generally found practical to have the officiating rabbi and cantor appointed as the witnesses. If two laymen are to be appointed, they should be so advised well in advance.

Exchange of Vows

There is no exchange of vows in the traditional ceremony; the exchange is implicit in the ritual itself. However, because of its widespread popularity, an exchange of vows is now included in many Reform and Conservative ceremonies. The accepted Reform text is:

Do you _____ take _____ to be your wife (husband), promising to cherish and protect her (him), whether in good fortune or in adversity, and to seek together with her (him) a life hallowed by the faith of Israel?

An accepted text for Conservative ceremonies is:

Do you _____ take _____ to be your lawful wedded wife (husband), to love, to honor, and to cherish?

Address to the Bride and Groom

It is considered proper, though by no means essential, for the rabbi to address the couple briefly in the course of the ceremony. There is no set formula, of course, for such an address, though it is common for the rabbi to offer homiletic interpretations of Biblical verses pertaining to marriage, to the attributes of a good wife and husband, and to the establishment of a Jewish home.

Circling the Groom

At some Orthodox ceremonies, the bride is required to walk around the bridegroom when she comes under the canopy in commemoration of the verse, "A woman shall go around a man" (Jeremiah 31:22). Most often she is led in procession around him seven times, corresponding to the seven different verses in the Bible which state, "and when a man takes a wife." At some weddings she circles the groom three times, corresponding to the three repetitions of the phrase, "And I will betrothe thee unto me" in the Book of Hosea (2:21-22).

HEBREW OR ENGLISH

The language of the traditional wedding service is Hebrew, as it is of most Jewish rituals. However, some English is now used to a greater or lesser degree depending on the preferences of the rabbi. Even when the ceremony is conducted largely in English, the groom is urged to recite the ancient formula of giving the ring in Hebrew. He may repeat the formula as prompted by the rabbi or, if he prefers, may recite it from memory unaided. Frequently, rabbis require the groom to recite the English version of the formula as well.

VI
The
Reception

לֵךְ אֱכֹל
בְּשִׂמְחָה
לַחְמֶךָ

GO EAT YOUR BREAD
WITH GLADNESS
AND DRINK YOUR WINE
WITH A JOYOUS HEART.

ECCLESIASTES 9:7

The reception following the ceremony is the time for rejoicing with the bridegroom and the bride. Traditionally, this phase of the wedding was called the *se'udah*, or meal—and quite a meal it was. In the Jewish communities of eastern Europe, it was natural to invite all one's relatives, close and distant, down to the smallest tot. The mothers of the couple and other relatives and friends were busy for days beforehand, baking and cooking delicacies for the feast.

In smaller communities, it was not uncommon for the whole town to be invited. And among well-to-do families there were two wedding feasts, one for family and friends, the other, the paupers' feast. The poor of the neighborhood would be invited to a special meal, either early on the wedding day or before. They were seated at a table with the bride and groom, and the parents of the couple waited on them. The bride and groom took turns dancing with them, and ended the meal by distributing coins.

In this manner, the families of the couple demonstrated their gratitude for their good fortune by providing food for those less fortunate. In our own day, this tradition often takes the form of contributions to a synagogue or a charity in honor of the couple.

The meal following a marriage ceremony is not an ordinary *se'udah*, but a *se'udat mitzvah*, a meal that accompanies the fulfillment of a religious commandment. Marriage is one such occasion; a *brit milah*, a circumcision, is another. The customary blessings and Grace are recited, with the addition of special blessings appropriate to the event.

Many Jews still follow the tradition of the wedding *se'udah*, the full meal for which all the guests are comfortably seated. Others are turning to different forms of entertaining, such as receptions of various types at which the guests may or may not be seated. But even at such receptions, it is possible to observe all the rituals of a wedding meal.

A wedding reception can take many forms. It can be large or small, lavish or simple, catered or homemade. No matter what its characteristics, however, it should reflect the tastes and style—and the pocket—of the hosts.

The most popular forms of reception are:

1. A dinner or luncheon served to seated guests
2. A buffet luncheon or dinner with sufficient tables for all guests, or one or two tables for bridal party and older guests
3. A tea reception: small sandwiches, fruit salads, punch, coffee, tea, wedding cake; tables for all guests, or just a bridal table
4. A cocktail reception: varieties of hors d'oeuvres, champagne, wedding cake, coffee; tables for all guests, or just a bridal table

THE CATERED AFFAIR

Confidence in a caterer is extremely important, not only for the hosts' peace of mind, but because they will have to trust his judgment in many matters. While a caterer's primary function is to provide food for the reception, he is often in a position to help with many other matters. He may recommend a florist, an orchestra, or a stationer for the invitations. He may, in fact, be able to handle all aspects of the wedding, and relieve the hosts of many trying details.

At the very outset, the hosts must inform him of how much they intend to spend; he will then let them know what he can provide for the stipulated amount.

AT A SYNAGOGUE

If a reception is to be held in a synagogue that has an established catering plan, the hosts will be given the name or names of the caterers who service that particular synagogue, and should arrange to meet with the caterer as early as possible. In many synagogues, the wedding date is not considered final until a contract has been signed with the caterer. It is important, however, to make arrangements with the synagogue authorities first.

At Orthodox and Conservative synagogues, only kosher food is served. Some Reform synagogues have only kosher facilities; others have both kosher and nonkosher facilities.

At a Hotel, Club, or Other Establishment

Commercial establishments generally have resident caterers. Some are strictly kosher. Those that are not may permit a kosher caterer to come in for a specific affair. The kosher caterer brings his own dishes, silver, linens, and even stoves. All the equipment is carried in trucks, and can be set up to serve any number of people. Some caterers have been known to transport meals and equipment hundreds of miles.

Some establishments have catering that is called "kosher style." This means that traditional Jewish foods are served, but the dietary laws are not followed, and the kitchen is not ritually supervised.

At Home

Caterers, both kosher and nonkosher, can provide any kind of reception for a home wedding. If necessary, they can bring dishes, silver, tables and chairs, and any other equipment that is needed.

In many communities there are caterers who do only the cooking—generally in the hosts' home—and manage the serving of the food. Very often they have their own assistants, waitresses, and bar men. After the menu is decided upon, the caterer gives the hosts a list of the foods to be purchased.

When a caterer of this kind is used, the hosts have to handle all the details, apart from the food, by themselves. This requires good organization, but it may reduce the cost of the wedding considerably.

Making Arrangements with the Caterer

No matter how good the caterer, the style, the choice of foods, and the embellishments should reflect not his taste, but that of the hosts. The caterer is an expert in his field, and he knows what is currently fashionable, but the ultimate decisions must be made by those who are giving the wedding.

Too many caterers sell a great abundance and variety of foods, claiming that this is impressive, and do not take into account the preferences of people who want to eat well, but wisely too. There are hosts who, having paid the caterer's highest price, insist that only half the number of dishes they are entitled to be served to the guests. This, they feel, is the only way they can be sure of having an affair that is elegant but not ostentatious.

The hosts should determine exactly what is to be included in the cost of the reception. Very often the wages for the waiters, the hat-check girl, and the *mashgiakh* (the supervisor of *kashrut*) are included in the price, but those for the manager and head waiter are not. Unless this is clarified beforehand, the hosts may find themselves after the wedding with an unexpected request for payment.

Generally not included in the cost of the reception are cigars and cigarettes, flowers, liquor, and souvenirs—monogrammed matchbooks, stirrers, ashtrays with the guests' names, and so forth. Despite claims to the contrary, the latter items generally detract from the elegance of the event, and can easily be dispensed with.

The caterer will, of course, want to know exactly how many guests will be present. He may ask for a guarantee of a minimum number and then grant the hosts up until a day or two before the wedding to make additions.

Special Arrangements for Kosher Food

There are kosher caterers in all large cities, and even in some smaller ones. But there are many parts of the country where such facilities are not available. The only way to have a kosher meal may be to prepare it in a home or a synagogue kitchen. The alternative would be to have a nonkosher caterer prepare a dairy meal with fish as the main course. He may have to be instructed in some of the requirements of *kashrut:* the varieties of fish permitted, the use of butter and vegetable fats only, the avoidance of products containing meat or meat derivatives.

Hosts who do not observe the dietary laws may be faced with the problem of whether or not to have a kosher wedding. They may have relatives and friends who observe *kashrut*, and do not wish to cause them embarrassment or discomfort by inviting them to a nonkosher reception. They may decide, in this case, to have a kosher reception.

If this is not feasible, the hosts will surely want to make special arrangements for those who observe the dietary laws. There are several ways in which this can be done. Cold foods such as fruits and vegetables, canned salmon, and cottage cheese will be eaten by nearly all who observe *kashrut*. Many will eat broiled fish, provided, of course, that it is a permissible species.

The serving of the meal will be facilitated if all who are to eat special food are seated together. If this cannot be done, the waiters should be told in advance which guests are to receive special food, so as to avoid embarrassing anyone.

Even though the dietary laws are not being observed, it would be wise to avoid serving those foods that are traditionally prohibited.

The hosts should bear in mind, too, that most Orthodox and Conservative rabbis will not attend a nonkosher dinner, even if special food is prepared for them. In some areas, rabbis will not officiate at a ceremony that is to be followed by a nonkosher reception.

MENUS

The choice of menus for a wedding reception is almost unlimited. While traditional Jewish dishes are certainly appropriate, any type of cuisine may be adopted. There are regional preferences to be taken into account as well as individual tastes.

In planning a reception, whether it involves a full meal or not, it is important to have a balanced menu of tasty, well-prepared dishes. The variety and quantity of dishes should be adequate but not overabundant.

The menus that follow are based on the observance of the dietary laws, according to which meat and dairy foods may not be served at the same meal. Though a festive kosher meal is usually a meat meal, there are times when a dairy meal is necessary, particularly if strictly kosher food is not available.

Apart from foods labeled "meat" or "dairy," there is another category, known as *pareve*, neutral. The foods in this category may be served with either meat or dairy meals, or alone. The following foods are *pareve:* fish (provided it has fins and scales), fresh, canned, or smoked; caviar, provided it is from a permissible fish; all vegetables; all fruits; and eggs. Synthetic cream and oleomargarine that contain no meat or milk products are now available, and are considered *pareve*.

Dinner or Luncheon Menus (*Meat*)

Supreme of Melons and Berries
Filet of Lemon Sole
Artichoke Hearts
Broiled Filet of Beef
Glazed Belgian Carrots   Petite Parsleyed Potatoes
Tossed Salad with Vinaigrette Dressing
Lemon Sherbet with Bing Cherries Melba
Petits Fours   Mints
Demitasse   Tea
Wedding Cake

Braised Sweetbreads
Chicken Broth with Noodles or Soup Nuts
Breast of Capon with Truffle Sauce
Asparagus Vinaigrette   Carrot Pudding
Avocado and Grapefruit Salad with French Dressing
Raspberry Sherbet on Brandied Peaches
Petits Fours   Mints
Demitasse   Tea
Wedding Cake

Pineapple Surprise
Chicken Broth with Miniature Matzo Balls
Roast Chicken
Noodle Pudding   Carrot Tzimmes
Asparagus
Choice of Relishes
Ice Cream (*pareve*) Molds with Chocolate Sauce
Demitasse   Tea
Wedding Cake

If the above menus are to be used for a luncheon, it is suggested that one course be eliminated.

Buffet Dinner or Luncheon Menu (*Meat*)

The menus above can be adapted to buffet service, assuming, of course, that the guests can be seated at small tables after helping themselves. Such a buffet might also include any of the traditional Jewish foods listed on page 101, or a selection from the following:

Chopped liver mold with crackers and party rye; meat blinis; *boeuf bourguignon;* brisket of beef; roast prime ribs of beef; tongue in apricot sauce with blanched almonds; fried chicken; chicken *cacciatore;* Cornish hen stuffed with wild rice; duck *à l'orange;* candied sweet potatoes; Italian green beans; broccoli; fruit salads

Dessert, pastries, demitasse, and wedding cake are a suitable conclusion for a buffet meal.

Cocktail or Tea Reception (Meat)

A choice of the following may be served:

Smoked salmon; gefilte fish balls; stuffed mushrooms; stuffed cabbage; franks in pastry dough; chopped liver; sautéed liver and mushrooms; miniature potato pancakes; meatballs in sweet and sour sauce; chicken salad; varieties of canapés; vegetable dip (hearts of celery, carrot sticks, cauliflower rosettes, radish roses, and avocado strips arranged in separate mounds, served with Russian dressing dip)

A sweet table, with pastries, nuts, and mints, a tea service, a coffee urn, and the wedding cake presiding over all, is a festive addition to this type of reception.

Dinner or Luncheon Menus (Dairy)

Fresh Fruit in Cantaloupe Basket
Filet of Sole Poached in White Wine
Peas and Pearl Onions
Tossed Salad
Rolls and Butter
Peach Melba
Nuts   Mints
Coffee
Wedding Cake

Creamed Soup
Cold Fresh Salmon with Dill Sauce
Asparagus   Parsleyed Potatoes
Rolls and Butter
Ice Cream Parfait
Nuts   Mints
Coffee
Wedding Cake

Buffet Dinner or Luncheon Menu (Dairy)

Choose from among the following:

Filet of sole *amandine;* poached salmon with hollandaise sauce; salmon mousse; halibut salad; gefilte fish; herring salad; egg salad; noodle pudding; beet and horseradish mold; cole slaw mold; string beans with mushrooms; green peppers stuffed with rice in tomato sauce; asparagus; tossed salad; fresh fruit salad; blintzes with sour cream; ice cream; pastries

Coffee and wedding cake put the finishing touches on this dairy buffet, which may be particularly effective in warm weather.

Cocktail or Tea Reception (Dairy)

Canapés, ribbon sandwiches, fried fish balls, deviled eggs, smoked salmon and whitefish; miniature potato pancakes; chopped herring with party rye; gefilte fish balls with horseradish dip; cheese puffs; assortment of cheese and crackers; stuffed mushrooms; vegetable dip (see page 99).

Desserts, coffee, tea, and wedding cake round out the menu for this reception—simple, but more than adequate.

A DESIGN FOR THE UNDERSTATED WEDDING

For people who prefer to entertain simply rather than on a grand scale; for people who want to invite all their friends and relatives to the *simḥa* and cannot do so with a dinner; and for people who have to keep the budget in mind, this menu may be just the answer:

Champagne or Punch
Petits Fours   Cookies
Nuts   Mints
Wedding Cake
Coffee

TRADITIONAL JEWISH FOODS

The menu for a Jewish wedding reception might well include one or more foods that we think of as traditional. Actually, they are traditional only in the sense that our forebears ate them in the countries of Europe from which they came. In many instances they are associated with holidays and with the Sabbath. The traditional dishes eaten by Jews in Morocco or Greece or Iraq are quite unknown to most American Jews—except those who come from a Sephardic background. Only in Israel do all the food traditions come together to form a kind of international Jewish cuisine.

Here, then, are some of the traditional Jewish foods that may be incorporated in a wedding menu:

Hors d'oeuvres. Gefilte fish; chopped liver; stuffed cabbage; calves-foot jelly; knishes (meat, potato).

Soup. Chicken, served with noodles, soup nuts (*mandlen*), or matzo balls; split-pea soup with marrow bones; borscht (hot or cold).

Entrée. Roast chicken, capon, duck, turkey, squab, beef.

Vegetables and other accompaniments. Carrot tzimmes, potato and prune tzimmes, noodle pudding (*kugel*), potato pudding, potato pancakes, kreplach, blintzes (filled with either meat or fruit), cholent, stuffed derma.

Desserts. Apple sauce; compote of dried fruits.

Cakes. Sponge, honey, nut; poppy-seed cookies; strudel filled with apples, fruits, or nuts; kichlach, teiglach.

Those foods that are associated with a particular holiday are frequently served at a wedding that takes place close to the holiday date:

Purim. Hamantaschen; kreplach.

Sukkot. Kreplach.

Ḥanukah. Potato latkes.

LEḤAYIM!

No wedding celebration is complete without wines and spirits, that which "gladdens the heart of man." What one serves may depend on the budget, on the facilities for serving, or purely on one's own evaluation of what is fitting.

The alcoholic beverages served at a wedding may fall into the following categories:

Punches only. A champagne punch and one made with fruit juices, wines, and liquors.

Champagne only.

Wine bar. Sauterne, Burgundy, sherry, champagne.

Fully equipped bar. Varieties of liquor, cocktails, champagne.

Wines and cordials. Served with and after meal.

A caterer will advise the hosts about the amounts needed. He may charge either by the bottle or per person. Sometimes the hosts decide to provide the liquor themselves, and the caterer supplies the set-ups. It is wise to check carefully into the exact costs and the amounts to be served, for this can be one of the most expensive items on the reception bill.

It is always considerate to provide a fruit punch or other nonalcoholic beverages for children and those adults who do not drink wine or liquor.

For a reception at which only champagne or punch is to be served, the following guide to quantities may be helpful:

One bottle of champagne (four-fifths of a quart) will serve seven to eight people, using three-ounce glasses

Two and one-half gallons of punch will serve fifty people, in six-ounce glasses

Religious Restrictions on Wines and Champagnes. Traditionally, the only wines or wine products considered kosher were those made and handled by Jews. The prohibition against using other wines originated in the days when the ancient Israelites lived among pagan peoples, who used wine as a libation to their gods. Even when Jews lived in Christian and Moslem countries, the prohibition was maintained. Today, it is observed by Orthodox and some Conservative Jews.

Reform Judaism has never accepted the prohibition. In Conservative Judaism, the rabbinate has ruled recently that the prohibition is no longer valid, and that the use of wine and champagne made under non-Jewish auspices is permitted.

Among all Jews, there is a sentimental attachment to the wines of the Holy Land. Israel exports a number of wines and champagnes, and their use is considered particularly appropriate at weddings and other religious occasions.

SEATING AND TABLE ARRANGEMENTS

Careful plans for table and seating arrangements are essential for a seated dinner or luncheon, and sometimes for a buffet reception as well.

In order for the seating of the guests to proceed smoothly, an exact blueprint must be worked out in advance. Start with a complete, alphabetized list of those who have accepted the invitation. Then draw up a plan of the room, showing placement of the bridal table and other tables. Will there be dancing during the meal? An area in the middle of the room must be left open. Be very sure to allow adequate space, not only for seating, but also for the comfortable passage of waiters between tables.

Number the tables on the blueprint, assigning even numbers to tables on the right and odd numbers to tables on the left. Arrange a set of large cards, each marked with the number of a table. Then, working back and forth between the guest list and the table plan, assign eight or ten guests (or whatever number the tables accommodate) to each table, noting the names on the card. When this is completed, mark the table number that has been assigned next to the name of each guest on the alphabetical list. It is often helpful to give a duplicate of this list to the caterer, head usher, or someone else who will assist with the seating of guests.

At large weddings, as each guest enters the reception room, he receives a small card showing his full name and table number. At the table, there may be individual place cards on which the names are written out, like this: "Miss Goodman," "Mr. Randall."

Who Sits Up Front

Deciding who is to sit where is not a routine matter. In some situations, in fact, the discussions on this subject may closely resemble a mediation meeting during a nationwide strike. Individual situations do vary, but in general, the closest relatives should be seated near the bridal table. If the number of guests is divided evenly between the bride's and groom's families, the seats up front should be divided accordingly. If there are fewer guests from one family, they will have fewer members at the front tables.

The attendants should also be seated near the bridal table, as should one's closest friends and elderly guests. Children are happier and much better off seated together, in a corner of the room where they can have greater freedom and privacy.

THE BRIDAL TABLE

The bridal table at a Jewish wedding often looks quite different from that at a non-Jewish wedding. Among Jews, it is customary to give precedence to the parents and grandparents of the bridal pair, and to seat them, not the attendants, with the bride and groom. The rabbi and cantor, with their wives, are also seated at the bridal table. The attendants are generally seated at a table close by. This practice is not in the realm of religious law, but it is a widely accepted custom, and one that has a great deal of warmth and appeal.

If there is room, the maid of honor and the best man might be included at the bridal table, especially if they are the only attendants.

If the table is not large, however, the rabbi and cantor and their wives and the grandparents may be seated nearby.

BUFFET RECEPTION

The same procedures for seating guests at a formal dinner may be used for a buffet reception. Place cards will probably be dispensed with, and perhaps table cards as well. A waiter or member of the family, armed with a list of table assignments, can be posted at the entrance to the reception to give each guest his table number.

If it is a cocktail or tea reception, at which the guests are usually not seated, it is still desirable to have a bridal table. In addition, it is always considerate to provide at least a few chairs, so that elderly guests can be seated.

DINNER FOR FIFTY GUESTS OR LESS

A large number of guests seated at many tables throughout a room is a pleasant sight, but when there are fewer than fifty guests, this arrangement may lack the desired sense of intimacy. It may be possible to arrange one large table that can accommodate up to fifty persons. This makes everyone feel as if he were sitting at the family dining table.

This can be done by placing two long tables parallel to each other to approximate a square. A table in the shape of a half circle is then placed at either end. This creates a lovely, large oval. Caterers and party rental firms have these tables.

NOTES ON DIFFERENT TYPES OF WEDDINGS

THE LARGE WEDDING

The large wedding, particularly the formal one, may require months of preparation. Of all the qualities needed to ensure its success, perhaps the most important is good organization. Because there are so many details involved, many people choose to engage a wedding consultant or social secretary, who will supervise all the arrangements. Such a person has often had considerable experience, and can not only take charge, but can help the hosts make all the necessary decisions.

Needless to say, there is a charge for the services of a professional consultant, and not everyone wishes to incur such an expense. For others the joy of arranging a wedding is one they do not care to miss, and so they prefer to do everything by themselves.

Since a large wedding requires so much organization, it may be helpful to list the various essential stages of the preparations. Here are the responsibilities of the bride and groom and their families:

Bride and Her Family

When the date has been set, reserve the synagogue, hotel, or hall. Inquire as to exact number of guests that can be accommodated. Also, set date for rehearsal.

Invite rabbi to officiate, and set date for premarital interview.

Prepare guest list, and list for announcements, if any. Get lists from groom's family.

Meet with caterer to plan reception.

Order invitations, announcements, informals with the bride's new name (and possibly some with her maiden name) and other needed stationery.

Select and invite wedding attendants.

Address and stamp envelopes for invitations and announcements (invitations to be mailed three to four weeks before wedding; announcements right after the wedding).

Order wedding outfits for bride, attendants, and mothers.

Shop for household and personal trousseau.

Engage photographer; make appointment to sit for bridal portrait.

Engage dance band for reception.

With groom, meet with cantor to discuss music for ceremony; if necessary, engage organist or other musicians.

Order Grace books and skullcaps.

Meet with florist to arrange decorations and flowers for the bridal party.

Purchase ring for groom, if he is to have one.

Select gifts for wedding attendants.

Take blood test.

Arrange accommodations for out-of-town attendants and guests.

Prepare wedding announcement for newspapers.

Choose wardrobe for wedding trip.

Groom and His Family

Invite attendants as soon as date and place are set.

If you will have an *Aufruf*, arrange date with synagogue.

Note dates for premarital interview and wedding rehearsal.

With bride, meet with cantor to discuss music for ceremony.

Shop for wedding outfit and personal wardrobe.

Buy wedding ring.

Make arrangements for wedding trip.

Apply for marriage license.

Take blood test.

Arrange bachelor dinner (if given by groom).

Order wedding flowers for bride, groom, groom's attendants, and groom's family.

Arrange accommodations for out-of-town attendants and guests.

Select gifts for attendants.

Prepare fees for rabbi, cantor, and others who you feel should receive remuneration.

THE SMALL WEDDING

Everyone seems to know what a large wedding is, but there are differences of opinion about what constitutes a small wedding. Under one hundred guests? Under fifty guests? Perhaps the answer is that small, when applied to weddings, can only be measured subjectively. If plans started out with a guest list of four or five hundred, and it was later decided to cut the list to two hundred, the hosts might well consider their wedding a small one. On the other hand, a family with very few relatives and a small circle of close friends might think of a wedding with fifty or seventy-five guests as large, or at least not small.

But there are differences between a large and a small wedding, and some objective guidelines are necessary. In general, a wedding that can take place in a chapel or in a home of moderate size may be considered small. There are usually fewer attendants at a wedding of this type. Apart from that, however, a small wedding can be exactly like a large one in its formality and in the details of the clothes, reception, flowers, and so forth. For many weddings considered small, the amount of preparation and details may well be the same as for a large wedding.

The exception to this, of course, is the very small wedding, which is attended only by the immediate families and possibly a few close friends. This wedding can be beautiful in every detail, but it will never involve as much preparation as a larger one.

Suggestions for handling various aspects of the small and very small wedding will be found throughout the book.

THE HOME WEDDING

Nothing can duplicate the warmth and intimacy of a wedding held in the home, particularly if it is the home in which the bride grew up. Since the biggest drawback to a home wedding, however, is lack of space, it is essential first to evaluate the potential guest list and the facilities of the home. It is worth consider-

ing, too, that a wedding at home means considerably more wear
and tear on the people who live there, not to speak of the furnish-
ings, rugs, and so forth. Once all these factors have been taken
into account, and the decision has been made in favor of the home
wedding, the wedding is already off to a good start, for the
environment and the atmosphere are in its favor.

The Ceremony. The ceremony for a home wedding is
exactly the same as that which takes place in a synagogue or
elsewhere. A *ḥuppah* may be borrowed from the synagogue or
constructed by a florist. It is possible, too, to make one's own,
using trellises covered with green leaves to which flowers may
be added. The location of the canopy depends on the proportions
and layout of the room or rooms to be used, but ideally it should
be placed so as to be seen clearly by all present.

If there is adequate room for seating the guests, the chairs
can be arranged so as to create an aisle leading to the canopy.
The florist might be asked to mark off an aisle with ropes or
white ribbon. This may be a useful idea even if the guests are to
stand. However, if there are no ropes and the guests are standing,
an usher asks the guests, minutes before the start of the ceremony,
to move to the sides of the room to create an aisle for the processional.

The bridal procession forms upstairs or in a room adjacent to
that in which the ceremony will be held. The bride and groom
generally have a maid of honor and a best man, though the
mother of the bride and the father of the groom can serve in
these capacities, if necessary.

In addition to the canopy, the following objects will be
needed for the ceremony:

A small table covered with a white cloth, placed under the
canopy or close to it
A decanter of wine
Two wine goblets (at Reform ceremonies, one)
A delicate glass wrapped in a napkin (if the breaking of the
glass is observed)

Though they are not required for the ceremony, the Sabbath
candlesticks that the bride will use in her own home may be
placed on the bridal table. A *kiddush* cup belonging to the groom
is often used as one of the wine goblets.

If skullcaps are to be worn, they will have to be provided by the hosts.

The Reception. The hosts may wish to engage a caterer who will not only provide the food, but also will arrange tables and chairs, take charge completely of the serving, bring waitresses and other help—in short, provide everything that is needed. Nevertheless, the bride's mother will still have to keep an eye on things, and make sure that the caterer and his staff carry out the prearranged plans.

For the home wedding that will not be handled completely by a caterer, there are several possibilities. The hostess can prepare all the food herself in advance, and store it in the freezer. Or, she may engage the services of a professional cook-caterer, who does all the cooking in the hosts' home, and may even take charge of the serving. The third possibility is to purchase prepared foods. One need only order everything for delivery on the day of the wedding. Whichever method is followed, the homemade reception can be as simple or elaborate as one wants. Everything depends on good organization and on the talents of the hostess.

When planning the home reception, it is well to bear in mind that adequate space will be needed for the bar or punch bowl. If the food is to be served buffet style, one large table will probably suffice for the food, though a separate table may be needed for coffee and desserts. These might even be served in another room. Provision should be made, as well, for coat racks or a separate coat room.

One room can be designated for the bridal party to meet in. The signing of the marriage contract can take place here, too.

The Garden Wedding

It may come as a surprise to predominantly urban Jews to learn that the outdoor wedding is an old Jewish custom. In the Middle Ages, the ceremony invariably took place in the courtyard of the synagogue. It was considered a good omen for the wedding to take place under the stars, so that the children of the couple would be "as numerous as the stars in heaven." To this day, the weddings of Hassidic Jews are held largely out-of-doors.

In parts of New York City, it is not uncommon to see a whole street blocked off for a mammoth Hassidic wedding. Since weather is sometimes an obstacle, there are wedding halls patronized by Hassidim that have a small opening in the ceiling so that the *mitzvah* of being married under God's canopy can still be observed. In Israel, which has an eight-month summer, most weddings take place out-of-doors.

In this country, the garden wedding, or any outdoor wedding, frequently has to contend with the elements. There are two ways in which the hosts can prepare for the worst. They can provide a large tent or canopy, which can even be heated, or they can make the necessary preparations for a last-minute change to the inside of the house.

But the plans for a garden wedding proceed on the assumption that the weather will be perfect. If possible, a shaded area should be used for the ceremony. If there is no natural foliage to serve as a backdrop, the florist can provide hedges or bushes or large urns of flowers. White ribbon on posts can be used to create an aisle, or the chairs can be arranged so as to create one.

There are times when it may be desirable to have a combination garden-home wedding. The ceremony might be held out-of-doors and the reception indoors, or the other way around. Such an arrangement can be helpful when space is limited.

A Canadian Wedding

Large weddings among Canadian Jews often follow a pattern that very nicely meets the needs of people who want to share their *simha* with as many friends and relatives as possible.

Family and closest friends are invited to the ceremony, and the dinner immediately following (perhaps with a cocktail hour preceding dinner). Dinner is served without interruption, that is, there is no dancing between courses. This means that more tables can be accommodated, and thus, more guests invited. After dinner, the Grace and the *Sheva Berakhot* are recited, followed by after-dinner speeches and toasts.

Only then does the dancing begin. If there is no other room for this purpose, the dinner tables are cleared away. At this time a second group of guests arrives, composed of the wider circle of the bridal couple's friends. A buffet table of liqueurs, sweets, fruits, and pastries is set up at one end of the room, and the party goes on!

Generally, two separate invitations are sent out for this type of wedding, one to those invited to the ceremony and dinner, the other to those invited to the reception after dinner. The first group might be invited to come at 6:30 P.M., the second group at 9:30 P.M.

RECEPTION ETIQUETTE FOR BRIDE AND GROOM

Once the ceremony is over, the bride and groom are apt to relax and to feel like kicking up their heels, but they may have to exercise a little restraint. There remains their obligation to their guests, some of whom may be meeting the bride or the groom for the first time. Apart from being the center of attention, the newlyweds will need plenty of patience and energy to mingle and talk with friends and family.

At a large wedding, the bride and groom either remain seated at the bridal table, so that guests may come up to them, or they circulate among the guests. If guests are seated for a dinner and there is dancing between courses, it delights everyone to have the bride and groom move from table to table, chatting with the guests.

Among the more Orthodox, the bride undoubtedly knows that it is considered improper for her to try to shake hands with male guests, and the non-Orthodox bride should bear this in mind, if there are members of the families or friends who observe this religious prohibition.

Here are a few pointers for the bride and groom, in their leading roles:

Stay seated when toasts are offered; only the guests rise.

Remain at the reception until all but the immediate families and the attendants have departed. In your eagerness to be off on your honeymoon, remember to say a warm good-by to all those who helped make the wedding such a wonderful event.

Write or telephone your families during the wedding trip, just to let them know that you are all right.

If possible, start acknowledging wedding gifts during the honeymoon, unless you are going off just for a weekend. This may seem unnecessary, but writing thank-you notes may be an even greater burden when you return and start setting up house.

VII
MUSIC, FLOWERS, AND PHOTOGRAPHS

THOU HAST CREATED JOY AND GLADNESS,
BRIDEGROOM AND BRIDE, MIRTH AND
EXULTATION, PLEASURE AND DELIGHT.

FROM THE MARRIAGE SERVICE

As every good hostess knows, attention to detail is essential for successful entertaining. This certainly applies to weddings, for though all eyes may be on the bride, the background contributes significantly to the desired mood of the occasion.

MUSIC AND DANCING

MUSIC FOR THE CEREMONY

Music is such an important part of a wedding that the bride and groom will surely devote much thought to choosing the selections, particularly for the ceremony itself. While the mere mention of this subject may evoke thoughts of traditional wedding marches, such as those by Wagner and Mendelssohn, the fact is that the range of possibilities is much wider, and frequently more interesting.

In every age and place, Jews have evolved their own customs concerning wedding music, frequently borrowing from their non-Jewish neighbors. In our own day, there are serious questions about the quality and appropriateness of much that is played at Jewish weddings. We are living in a period in which, literally, anything goes: tunes from Broadway shows such as *Fiddler on the Roof*, Israeli folk songs, avant-garde chamber music, liturgical compositions, Hassidic melodies, Mozart and Haydn, and "Here Comes the Bride," the latter, by the way, composed by an avowed anti-Semite! Some synagogues have taken a stand, and offer the couple specific guidelines, but for the most part, there are few restrictions.

In part, this is because it is difficult to formulate well-defined rules about what is fitting for a Jewish ceremony. Perhaps it would be helpful if people were to think not in terms of what is or is not Jewish music, but rather in terms of sacred and profane. Music that is associated with the theater, for example, even if composed by Jews, seems singularly out of place at a religious ceremony.

It is up to the bridal pair, therefore, to help set the musical mood. To accomplish this, they should bear in mind both their own tastes and the inherent nature of the occasion. Whether or not it takes place in a synagogue, the ceremony is both spiritual and joyous, and the music should reflect these qualities. In recent years, Jewish composers have begun to create modern music for the Jewish wedding, and at some future time, one or more of these compositions may well achieve popular acclaim. At present, however, it is necessary to consult a cantor for information and advice. He will be glad to tell you about some of the new wedding music or about traditional liturgical selections that are always appropriate. If you prefer chamber music or other compositions, you will certainly want to discuss your plans with the cantor.

When selecting music for the processional, try to picture it as a smooth, flowing whole. At a number of weddings, a different melody is played for each individual or group that comes down the aisle. This may be entertaining, but it definitely creates a choppy effect. A much lovelier mood is established when one composition accompanies the entire processional, or at least everyone but the bride. Her entrance is the climax, and different music might be introduced at that point.

Vocal selections before or during the ceremony are less popular than they once were. Many synagogues discourage the practice, probably because so many of the songs that are chosen are inappropriate in the sanctuary. The kind of sentimental ballad that is associated with weddings, and that invariably brings a tear to the eye, is better reserved for the reception.

Nevertheless, there are beautiful and appropriate vocal numbers, as well as incidental music, that can be offered with dramatic effect before the ceremony. Some of these compositions are listed below; others may be suggested by the cantor.

The music for the synagogue ceremony is usually provided by an organ or piano, or by string instruments, if the synagogue permits. The cantor or rabbi will be able to suggest qualified musicians who may be engaged for the occasion.

When the wedding takes place in a hotel or catering establishment, it is quite possible that the dance-band pianist will double as organist for the ceremony. While it is true that this is an economical arrangement, it is not always a satisfactory one. Frequently, the atmosphere of the dance band carries over to the choice of music for the ceremony and to the style in which it is played. One solution, probably the best, is to engage a synagogue organist for the occasion. If this is not feasible, the couple might wish to select their own music and, if necessary, purchase the actual scores and give them to the pianist-organist.

For a home wedding, any instruments or recordings may be used. Here, too, the musical selections must be chosen with care. The hosts may wish to rent a desk-size organ and to engage an organist. Or, if there is a piano in the home, the wedding is a perfect opportunity for a talented member of the family to show what he can do.

Although it would be impossible to list the complete repertoire of appropriate music for the Jewish ceremony, the suggestions that follow will provide a good picture of what is available and acceptable. A cantor can provide additional suggestions, as can the music publishers. (Key letters are the initials of the publishers from whom the music may be obtained. See page 125 for names and addresses.)

Complete Wedding Services

Cantorial Anthology, Volume V, compiled by Gershon Ephros. (B)

Music for a Modern Jewish Wedding, by Davidson, Helfman, Meisels, Miron, Secunda, and Weiner. (MM)

Music for the Jewish Wedding Ceremony, by R. Kosakoff. (T)

Vocal Solos

"Barukh Haba" and "Mi Adir," by Mario Castelnuovo-Tedesco. (MM)

"Set Me as a Seal upon Thy Heart," by H. Reznik. (T)

"I Will Betrothe Thee" and "A Woman of Valor," by S. Adler. (T)

"Eshet Hayil" ("A Woman of Valor"), by Ch. Davidson. (T)

"Ana Dodi," by M. Janowsky. (M)

"My Beloved and I," by R. Kosakoff. (T)

"Song of Ruth," by M. Goldman. (T)

"Du Un Ich," by A. Ellstein. (M)

"Mein Teiere," by I. Trilling. (M)

"Deine," by J. Rumshinsky. (M)

Music from the Song of Songs

A number of well-known Israeli songs with texts from the Song of Songs may be used as solos, or, if tastefully arranged, for the processional and recessional. Among these songs are:

"Dodi Li" ("My Beloved Is Mine"), "Hinach Yafa" ("Behold Thou Art Fair"), "Ana Dodi" ("Where Has My Beloved Gone"), "Iti Milvanon" ("Come with Me from Lebanon"), "Hana'ava Babanot" ("The Fairest among the Maidens"), "Kol Dodi" ("The Voice of My Beloved"). (M)

Additional compositions using passages from the Song of Songs have been written by a number of Israelis, particularly I. Miron, A. Boscovich, S. Levy, and N. Nissimov. (M) and (MM)

Organ Music

"Suite of Organ Pieces," by E. Fromm. (T)
"Four Wedding Marches," by E. Bloch. (S)
"Six Liturgical Pieces," by I. Fried. (T)
"Processional" and "From the World of My Father," by H. Berlinsky. (MER)
"Ceremonial Marches," by M. Weinberg. (MER)
"Organ Solos," by W. Brenner. (T)
"Six Preludes for Organ," by E. Bloch. (S)
Organ Music for Worship, compiled by S. Adler, including music by H. Adler, Jean Berger, A.W. Binder, E. Levy, H. Schalit, R. Starer, and others. (W)
From *The Union Hymnal:* Psalm 150, Psalm 24, and "Lekha Adonai Hagedulah." (UAHC)

Instrumental Solos

See "Instrumental Music," a pamphlet published by the Jewish Music Council of the National Jewish Welfare Board.

Music for the Reception

Whether you are engaging a society dance band or a lone accordionist, consider the music that is to accompany the reception as important as the bridal party's outfits, the reception menu, and all the other trimmings. The choice of instruments and the selections to be played should be in harmony with the over-all atmosphere of the event.

The size of the room or hall, and the number of guests, are factors to consider in determining the number and type of musicians, though in many areas the number may be prescribed by union agreements.

Choose an orchestra that has been highly recommended by someone whose opinion you value, or one that you have already heard and liked. If you are uncertain, ask the orchestra leader if you may come to hear his group perform at another event before making up your mind. Hotels and caterers almost always recommend dance bands, so you may find one you like this way.

By all means discuss the kind of music you want with the orchestra or ensemble leader. He will undoubtedly agree that the music should be audible, but should not make conversation a trial. Let him know the type of selections you like, both during the meal and for dancing. You might wish to give him a list of request numbers in advance to make sure that your favorites are included.

If you want Israeli and Jewish folk songs or folk music of another country, be sure to let him know. You might care to indicate that you want them played as folk songs and not as jazz.

Small Wedding. When the number of guests is small, a regular dance band may prove overpowering. Appropriate music, either for dancing or just for background, is best provided by a pianist, an accordionist, or a small string ensemble. At a home wedding, carefully selected records played on a fine stereo or hi-fi set can provide a pleasant musical background.

WEDDING ENTERTAINMENT

In great-grandmother's day, no wedding was celebrated without a *badḥen*, a professional bard who sang songs and rhymes directly related to the particular wedding and its principals. Frequently, the *badḥen* was learned as well as amusing, and his ditties were brilliant combinations of Jewish learning and wit. Unfortunately, the profession of *badḥen* has all but disappeared, and there are many who believe that we are the poorer for it.

A kind of substitute, of course, is the master of ceremonies, and at many large weddings the orchestra leader assumes this role. Whether or not he is to do so, however, is a matter for the hosts to decide. The standard procedure is for the band leader to provide a triumphant fanfare heralding the entry of bride and groom into the reception, to announce the first dance of the newlyweds, and to preside over the cutting of the wedding cake. If he fancies himself a comedian, he might also offer a little humor, tasteful or otherwise.

An alternative is to designate a member of the family—someone who is at home in front of an audience—as master of ceremonies. His knowledge of the family, of the backgrounds of the bride and groom, of little-known facts about their courtship, and so forth, can provide fun for all in an atmosphere of great warmth.

Among Jews in Canada and Great Britain, a member of the family almost always serves as toastmaster. Quite often it is the father of the bride. During the meal or after it, he welcomes his guests and then calls on several others to say a few words. Among those who might be called on are the groom's father, the rabbi, a grandfather, or a near relative or close friend who is prominent in the community. The best man is called on to offer the first toast to the couple. Then the groom rises to toast the bride. All this provides just the right amount and kind of entertainment to enliven what is otherwise just a cut-and-dried dinner.

Dancing

It is customary for the bride and groom to dance the first dance with each other, and this is always a beautiful moment. The bride's father might cut in on this dance, and then perhaps the groom's father, while the groom dances first with his mother and then with his mother-in-law. There are many different ways to arrange this part of the dancing, but it is customary for the guests to wait until the couple, their parents, and the attendants have had a whirl around the floor.

Apart from social dances, Israeli folk dances, such as the *horah*, and traditional East European circle dances, contribute fun and spirit to a Jewish wedding. At very Orthodox weddings these, in fact, are the only dances, since men and women are not permitted to dance with each other. For the traditional Jewish dances, no one need be a wallflower, and since the precise steps are unimportant, there is no excuse not to join in!

Among the very Orthodox, men and women form separate circles for dancing, or men dance with men and women with women. The one exception is the *Kosher Tantz*, which is reserved for the newlyweds and their closest relatives. The bride and groom take turns dancing with both male and female relatives; since men and women may not hold hands, however, they hold opposite corners of a handkerchief between them.

In the *Mitzvah Tantz*, guests revolve around the bride, who dances briefly with individuals in the center, or the guests simply dance around the bride, who is seated on a chair. As the momentum builds, a group of strong males often lift the chair, with the bride on it, and whirl her around.

The *Heidim Deidim* is danced by two men who face each other and entwine right arms. Many such couples dance about the room, kicking their legs high in the air, to traditional melodies. It is a dance of great enthusiasm as the men spin about, snapping their fingers and joining their voices to the music.

A beautiful old custom concerns the mother of the bride or groom who may be marrying off the last of her children. She is seated on a chair in the middle of the room and is crowned with a circlet of flowers. The guests dance around her in a large circle, to traditional melodies or to a popular Yiddish song called *Die Mezinke Ausgegeben* ("The Youngest Has Been Given Away"). This is not only a beautiful ceremony, but a real tribute to a mother who has raised a family and brought them all to the marriage canopy.

FLOWERS

The beauty and fragrance of fresh flowers provide a festive accent at a wedding and dress up the entire occasion. This does not mean that the greater the quantity, the lovelier the effect, for here, too, good taste and a sense of proportion are crucial.

In a synagogue, particularly, it is important not to overwhelm the innate beauty of the sanctuary and the ark with too many flowers and greens. Many synagogues have regulations limiting the amount and types of floral decorations that may be used. If there are no regulations, bear in mind the size of the pulpit and the colors of the synagogue decor when planning with the florist. Large and airy ferns at both sides of the *ḥuppah* together with large candelabra filled with many candles are a most effective arrangement. (Make sure, however, that fire regulations do not prohibit lighted candles.)

Sometimes the florist suggests to the hosts that massing the table centerpieces on the pulpit is an economical way to fill the synagogue with flowers. This works out well in some instances, but for the most part it results in a flower show, not subtle decoration. It is not necessary to fill the synagogue with flowers; most often a single bouquet on the pulpit is enough to create a lovely setting.

It is wise, too, to avoid arrangements that look unnatural in the synagogue setting. Trellises, swinging garden gates, white, wrought-iron fences, and similar creations may be effective in a home or a hotel ballroom, but are quite out of place in the sanctuary.

Flowers sprayed with color to conform to the color scheme of the wedding are another offense. If nature created white mums, for example, why improve on nature by coloring them blue?

Small bouquets may be used to ribbon off the center aisle, and these are usually attached to the ends of the pews. Pedestals or tall flower-and-candle containers can also be used on the aisle, but care should be exercised lest they narrow the aisle or obstruct the view of the guests.

If a small wedding is taking place in a large synagogue, the effect of emptiness can be overcome by creating a hedge of greens around the pews that are being used. Concentrated light on this small area can add to the illusion of a small chapel.

For a home or hotel wedding, the florist can create a simple setting for the ceremony, using tall stands filled with ferns and flowers behind and at the sides of the canopy. If there is no canopy, the stands are used to mark off the area in which the ceremony takes place. If the room is a large one, an aisle can be created with white ribbons or rope attached to white stands, with or without bouquets and candles.

An old-fashioned choice that is becoming popular again is the combination of white flowers with green ferns and other leaves. This is always effective, though floral arrangements at weddings run the gamut of all the colors in nature's palette. The pale pinks shading to deeper American Beauty tones are very popular. Yellow and white is another attractive combination, and can be used well with gold or white tablecloths at the reception. The florist can suggest many other possibilities.

A wise choice may be to use whatever flowers are in season. This not only provides a tasteful setting that is in tune with nature, but it may be more economical.

The Huppah (Canopy)

A recent article on the high cost of weddings mentioned that more money is spent on flowers at Jewish weddings than at non-Jewish weddings because "the canopy must be adorned with flowers." Alas, the writer was only repeating a popular misconception. The traditional canopy is a velvet or satin cloth supported by four poles, either held by four men or fixed in special holders on the floor. Greens and flowers *may* be used to decorate the canopy, but they are by no means mandatory. What has become popular in recent years, particularly at Reform weddings, is a floral canopy, one made entirely of greens and flowers. This can be magnificent in the right setting, but it does cost a good deal, with prices starting at about one hundred and fifty dollars.

A white carpet for the center aisle is generally provided by the florist, and is ribboned off so that no one may walk on it before the processional begins.

The Reception

The colors used for the flowers at the ceremony are often repeated in the reception decorations. Small centerpieces on the guests' tables and more elaborate ones on the bridal table add a festive touch, no matter how simple or elaborate the reception. A centerpiece should be light and delicate in feeling so as to highlight each beautiful flower, and low enough so that those at the table may see each other.

For an evening wedding, candles are a perfect complement to a floral centerpiece. They might also be used during the day, if there is little or no natural light in the room.

Flowers for the Bridal Party

It is customary for the bride to carry a small bouquet or a white Bible covered with a few choice flowers. The bridal flowers are usually white. Sometimes the bouquet or flower arrangement is made up with a going-away corsage set in its center. This is removed when the bride and groom are ready to leave the reception.

For the bride who is not dressed in white, flowers in the same color as her dress, or in complementary shades, are appropriate.

White boutonnieres are worn by the best man, the ushers, and the fathers and grandfathers of the bridal pair. The groom, too, wears a boutonniere, but his must be slightly different from those worn by the other men. Very often, a flower or flowers from the bridal bouquet form the groom's boutonniere.

The bridesmaids carry identical bouquets in shades that match or complement their dresses. The bouquet for the maid of honor differs slightly from that of the bridesmaids.

Corsages may be provided for the mothers and grandmothers of the bride and groom. Sometimes an aunt or very dear friend who has been particularly close to the bride or groom may also be presented with a corsage. This is a small gesture, but it expresses warm recognition of her loving role in the family.

Not all costumes are enhanced by the addition of corsages. The gowns and hats worn by the mothers of the bridal pair may be so intricately worked with lace, beading, or other trimming that flowers would detract from their beauty. In such cases, the mothers might prefer to have no flowers, or to carry simple bouquets or sheaves of long-stemmed flowers.

The flower girl carries a basket of rose petals, which she strews along the aisle in front of the bride. If this is not desirable, the flower girl may simply carry a very pretty, miniature nosegay or basket of flowers.

PHOTOGRAPHS

Is there anyone who does not cherish the one photograph, now yellowed and crumbling at the edges, that his grandparents or great-grandparents took at their wedding? Until very recently, that single photograph was all most couples had to remind them of their wedding day. But we live in an age in which nearly everyone is adept with not one, but several, types of cameras, and in which professional photographers promise to capture every glorious moment of the wedding day. Now the bride and groom have hundreds of pictures to pass on to the next generations. But there is a price to pay, and it is not only financial.

Every moment spent posing for pictures is a moment stolen from participation in the wedding festivities. Just as important, it can be physically exhausting to be on camera for any stretch of time. There is also the fact that professional picture-taking necessitates a good deal of equipment and lights, and not everyone enjoys bumping into photographers and their gear at every turn. All in all, extensive and complicated photography can make a shambles of a wedding, and the hosts should give careful consideration to their real needs before embarking on a major photographic operation.

For most couples, a good selection of pictures would include a number of formal, posed shots of the bride and groom, the immediate families, and the bridal party, as well as some candid shots of certain key moments during the day. These may be slides or regular photos, in black and white or color, and they may, if you so choose, be put together in a beautiful album to serve as a memento of the day.

It is, of course, not necessary to spend exorbitant amounts of money on photographs. When economy is a factor, or when those concerned do not wish more than a few pictures, it might be best to ask a close friend or relative who is handy with a camera to take a roll or two of film.

Photographing the Ceremony

Religious authorities generally do not look with favor on photography during a religious service or ceremony. Even the gentle click-click of one camera, not to speak of noisier equipment and flash bulbs, detracts from the dignity and reverence of the occasion. If the wedding is to take place in a synagogue, it is quite possible that there are restrictions on picture-taking during the ceremony. Sometimes permission is granted for a time exposure, using the existing light, to be taken from a balcony or other inconspicuous vantage point. For the most part, though, pictures in the sanctuary must be taken after the ceremony, if at all. The participants in the processional may be photographed just before they enter the sanctuary and as they exit from it during the recessional.

Hotels and catering halls may not have such reservations about photographing the ceremony, but the officiating rabbi may, so check with him before making arrangements with the photographer. As in a synagogue, pictures may be taken of the bridal party as they enter and leave the hall.

Selecting a Photographer

Finding the right photographer, in terms of your budget and the kind and quality of the pictures you want, takes careful shopping. Get recommendations from friends and relatives, but be sure to see samples of the photographer's work before making a decision. If you are shopping via advertisements or the telephone directory, try to visit the studios that merit serious consideration. If you simply telephone, the studio may suggest sending a representative to your home, and you may then feel obliged to repay such service with a commitment.

Seek quality rather than quantity, and don't be swept off your feet by a tempting offer of more for your money. In the long run, fewer photographs of top quality will yield much greater satisfaction.

The same caution should apply to recommendations which the caterer or hotel may offer. Using the photographer they suggest may save you time and energy, but be sure to examine samples first.

How You Can Help the Photographer

Though the success of your wedding pictures rests largely on the skill of the photographer, there are a number of things you can do to make his work easier and more effective.

All women in the bridal party should be advised to apply make-up with a light touch. Bear in mind, however, that iridescent make-up, white and pale shades, or lipsticks and eye liners that contain white do not photograph well. Black and brown eye liners are recommended for best results. Make-up that covers circles under the eyes and wrinkles should be covered with a powder base and powder.

It is not always necessary to photograph the women holding their bouquets, and in fact, too many flowers tend to overwhelm a picture and detract from the people themselves.

Work out a careful time schedule for picture-taking, and notify everyone concerned. If you want glossies of a bridal portrait to send to the newspapers, arrange for a sitting in advance of the wedding day, either in your own home or at the shop where you purchase your gown, when you go for the last fitting. For pictures to be taken at home before you leave for the wedding, allow at least an hour, and make arrangements for getting dressed accordingly. If pictures are to be taken only at the place of the wedding, ask the photographer and all those to be photographed to be there at least an hour before the start of the ceremony. Make a list, if necessary, of the group photos you want, and designate one member of the family to gather the subjects in one place and help pose them.

TAPE-RECORDING THE CEREMONY

Though a photographic record of the ceremony may not be possible, there is generally no objection to tape-recording the event. It can be done by a member of the family who is experienced with the equipment, or by a professional using his own equipment.

Music Publishers

T	Transcontinental Music Publications
	1674 Broadway, New York, N.Y.
MM	Mills Music, Inc.
	1619 Broadway, New York, N.Y.
MER	Mercury Music
	17 West 60th Street, New York, N.Y.
S	G. Schirmer, Inc.
	609 Fifth Avenue, New York, N.Y.
B	Bloch Publishing Company
	31 West 31 Street, New York, N.Y.
M	Metro Music Company
	54 Second Avenue, New York, N.Y.
W	Wallan Music Company
	1841 Broadway, New York, N.Y.
UAHC	Union of American Hebrew Congregations
	838 Fifth Avenue, New York, N.Y.

National Jewish Welfare Board
145 East 32nd Street, New York, N.Y.

VIII

RITUALS
AND CUSTOMS

וארשתיך לי בצדק

I WILL BETROTH THEE UNTO
ME IN RIGHTEOUSNESS. HOSEA
2:19

A series of religious rituals and customs precedes and follows the wedding. Each helps prepare the bride and groom for their new life and their new place in the community.

AUFRUF

Although the bride is usually the center of attention in all the fuss leading up to a wedding and at the wedding itself, Judaism reserves a special moment, a special ritual, for the groom alone. This is the *Aufruf* (a German word meaning "calling up"*), when the groom is called to the reading of the Torah and recites the same blessings he first recited when he was Bar Mitzvah. This practice is followed by Orthodox and Conservative Jews.

The *Aufruf* may take place at any service at which the Torah is read, which usually means on the Sabbath or a Monday or Thursday morning. Most often, the *Aufruf* is scheduled for the Sabbath immediately before the wedding, but it may be held on any convenient date. The rabbi should, of course, be consulted before a date is set.

When the groom is called to the Torah, he chants the customary blessings. If the groom is sufficiently learned, he may also be honored with the *Haftarah*, the chanting of a portion from Prophets, which follows the Torah reading. In some synagogues, the rabbi then asks the bride to join the groom on the pulpit, and he recites a special prayer blessing their forthcoming marriage.

In some Orthodox circles, a very old custom is still practiced: the women in the synagogue shower the groom with raisins and nuts when he recites the blessings, undoubtedly as an omen of fertility.

Synagogue Arrangements. It is customary for the *Aufruf* to be held in the synagogue with which the groom and his family are affiliated, but if this is impractical, it may be held in the synagogue of the bride's family. If neither family has a syna-

---

* In Yiddish, *Ufruf*. No English term for the ceremony has ever achieved popular usage.

gogue affiliation, the groom can make the arrangements with any local synagogue, or seek the assistance of the rabbi who will officiate at the wedding.

It is not amiss for the groom or his parents to send a contribution to the synagogue after the *Aufruf* has taken place.

Invitations. The bride and her family, the groom's family, and a small number of close relatives and friends may be invited to the *Aufruf.* (If any of the guests are not Jewish, it would be courteous to explain in advance that the men are expected to wear skullcaps, as at the wedding itself. The *tallit,* prayer shawl, is of course worn only by Jews.)

The invitation is generally informal—either a handwritten note or a telephone call from the groom's mother. If a reasonably large group is to be invited, a small printed invitation may be sent:

> We cordially invite you to worship with us at the Sabbath morning service at the Sons of Israel Synagogue, North Main Street, St. Louis, on August 22nd, 1964. At this service our son, David, will be called up for an *Aliyah* on the occasion of his approaching marriage to Barbara Lesser.
>
> Lester and Evelyn Kaplan
>
> Kiddush luncheon following the service
>
> R.S.V.P.

Dress. Attendance at an *Aufruf* requires no special attire, and both men and women wear what they would normally wear to a synagogue service. For the bride, a suit or a daytime dress with sleeves, and a hat are appropriate.

The Kiddush. It is customary, though by no means obligatory, for the groom's family to provide a *kiddush* for the congregation after the *Aufruf.* The *kiddush* may consist simply of wine and cake, or it may be a seated luncheon. Customs concerning this *kiddush* vary in different parts of the country, but in general it is a simple affair, and elaborate menus are avoided. Though any kind of food may be served, traditional Jewish dishes are always appropriate—and welcome!

For a Sabbath *Aufruf,* it must be remembered that observant Jews will not eat foods cooked on the Sabbath. The menu should include only cold dishes, or foods that are prepared in advance and kept warm or heated slowly. Here are some sample menus:

1. Wine, cookies and cake (sponge and honey cakes are most often served).

2. Wine, liquor, cakes, gefilte fish, herring tidbits, crackers, salads.

3. Wine, liquor, cakes, gefilte fish, noodle pudding, fresh fruit.

4. Varieties of hors d'oeuvres, wine, liquor, punch, cakes.

5. Seated luncheon: gefilte fish or fruit cup, roast chicken, noodle pudding, carrot tzimmes, tossed salad, dessert, cake and coffee (served with non-dairy cream) and tea.

6. Buffet meat luncheon: gefilte fish, chopped liver, cold roast beef, rolled cabbage, sweetbreads, potato or noodle pudding, carrot tzimmes, fruit molds, tossed salad, wines, liquor, cakes, coffee and tea.

For an elaborate *kiddush*, a large, uncut *ḥallah* should be on the table, and should be covered until the time comes to cut it. When the *ḥallah* is present, the repast then is considered a meal, and the Blessing over Bread and the Grace after Meals are recited.

A wine bottle and *kiddush* cup should also be provided.

Weekday Aufruf. A weekday morning synagogue service is held early, usually before nine o'clock, and it lasts less than an hour. It is customary to provide the worshipers with wine and cake following the service. Coffee, too, is always appreciated this early in the morning.

If a more substantial menu is wanted, any of the following would be fine:

1. Wine, cake, orange juice, rolls, smoked fish, coffee.

2. Wine, cake, juice or fruit, varieties of fish, scrambled eggs, bread and rolls, coffee.

3. For a brunch: all of the dishes in menu #2, plus blintzes or noodle pudding.

Arrangements for a *kiddush* in the synagogue are usually made with the sexton or other official who can advise you about the number of people to expect at a Sabbath or a weekday service.

Kiddush at Home. Sometimes a simple *kiddush* is provided for all the worshipers in the synagogue, followed by a more substantial meal at home for invited guests. The rabbi, cantor, and sexton should be invited; if it is for a Sabbath luncheon, their wives are included in the invitation. Needless to say, they are invited only if kosher food is served, and if the Sabbath is observed strictly—no smoking and no music, for example. The hosts provide skullcaps and Grace books.

Gifts. An old and beautiful tradition calls for the bride to present her groom with a *tallit* (prayer shawl) to be worn at his *Aufruf* and thereafter. The new *tallit* gives evidence of his new role as head of a household. The bride of the past would lovingly embroider a velvet bag for the *tallit*, with the groom's Hebrew initials, a wreath of flowers, and perhaps a quotation from the Bible. Today's bride may do the same, though she is probably more inclined to purchase one, of either American or Israeli manufacture.

A *kiddush* cup makes an appropriate gift to the *ḥatan* from the bride's parents or grandparents, and the groom's family might wish to use the occasion to present the *kallah* with a beautiful pair of candlesticks. Both the *kiddush* cup and the candlesticks might then be used at the wedding ceremony, a most meaningful way to initiate their use.

Prayer for the Betrothed

Reform Jews have a special ceremony, which usually takes place at a Friday night service, shortly before the wedding date. The following prayer for the bride and groom is recited by the rabbi:

> Loving Father, grant Thy blessing to _____ and _____, who come into Thy sanctuary to thank Thee for the gift of their love. They seek Thee, O God, in joy, and they pray that Thou wilt look with favor upon their union. Hopefully they look forward to the day when, under Thy protection, they may establish a home within the Jewish community.
>
> Teach them, O God, that unless Thou dost build the house, they who build it labor in vain. Hallow their love, bind their lives together, and help them to face the future with trust in each other, and with faith in Thee. Sustain them in every trial and temptation. In Thy grace, join them unto each other with a love that shall not falter, and cause them to approach their marriage with understanding hearts and consecrated spirits.

HONORING THE MEMORY OF DECEASED PARENTS

It is only natural that a bride or groom who has lost a parent should experience his sense of loss anew as the wedding day draws near. In the Jewish tradition, it is customary for the bereaved son or daughter to visit the grave of the departed parent before being married, and to recite the memorial prayer for the dead, *El Malei Rahamim.* If a visit to the grave is not feasible, the bride or groom may attend a Monday or Thursday morning synagogue service, at which time the Torah is read, and ask that the memorial prayer be recited.

A belief persists in some circles that the prayer for a departed parent should be recited as part of the wedding ceremony. Most rabbis, however, discourage this practice, pointing out that a note of sorrow and mourning should not be allowed to mar the joyousness of the wedding. There is "a time to weep and a time to laugh; a time to mourn and a time to dance," said Ecclesiastes, and this view is aptly applied to the present situation.

RITUAL IMMERSION FOR THE BRIDE

The *mikvah,* or ritual bath, occupied a place of prominence in the Jewish community of old. It was particularly important for the woman, who was required to cleanse herself of the periodic impurity resulting from her menstrual flow before resuming sexual relations with her husband. The woman about to be married was introduced to the *mikvah* and to the ceremony of immersion prior to her wedding so that she entered marriage in a pure state.

Today, the laws of family purity, as they are called, are observed by Orthodox and some Conservative Jews. Ritual baths are maintained by large Jewish communities, and here and there by smaller ones.

The bride who plans to observe the laws of family purity must arrange to visit the *mikvah* at an appropriate time before her wedding. Because the laws governing ritual purification are so complex, she should consult a rabbi for specific guidance and instruction. She will also want to read any of a number of good books and pamphlets on the subject, among them: "Jewish Family Life, The Duty of the Woman," by Rabbi Sidney B. Hoenig. This pamphlet is available from the Union of Orthodox Jewish Congregations of America, 84 Fifth Avenue, New York, N.Y.

FASTING ON THE WEDDING DAY

Among Orthodox and some Conservative Jews, the bride and groom fast on the wedding day until after the ceremony. The wedding day is considered a day of atonement, like Yom Kippur. The bride and groom fast as a means of purification, so that they may enter their new life cleansed of past sins, and, in fact, reborn. In addition to fasting, confessional prayers are recited.

Fasting is prohibited on the Sabbath, and on the holidays of Ḥanukah, Purim, Lag B'Omer, and Tu B'Shevat, and on *Rosh Ḥodesh* (the first day or two days of a new Hebrew month). Should a wedding date fall on any of these days, the bride and groom do not fast.

MAY THE BRIDE AND GROOM SEE EACH OTHER BEFORE THE CEREMONY?

Every tradition has superstitions to the effect that it is bad luck for the bride and groom to see each other on the wedding day, before the ceremony. There is, of course, no foundation for these beliefs, and in Judaism, there is no serious objection to the bride and groom seeing each other. Many authorities do discourage it, though, on the grounds that the novelty of being together is enhanced if the couple wait until they meet under the canopy.

VEILING THE BRIDE

The bridal veil originated, we are told, with the Matriarch Rebekah. When she was brought to marry Isaac, she covered herself with a veil as she approached the tents of her bridegroom. From that day on, the veil has been the universal symbol of bridal modesty.

An old and beautiful custom is the ceremony of veiling the bride by the groom (in Yiddish, *Badeken,* meaning "to cover"), which takes place before the wedding service, usually in conjunction with the signing of the *ketubah.* It is practiced at Orthodox and some Conservative weddings. It may take place in the rabbi's study or in the bride's room. Generally, only the immediate families, the maid of honor, and the best man attend.

It is not clear why this ceremony was introduced into our tradition, but it may have had something to do with the fact that marriages were arranged, and the groom, having had little opportunity to see his wife-to-be before the wedding, wanted to make certain that he was marrying the girl promised him.

The ceremony usually begins with the signing of the *ketubah* by two witnesses, and at some ceremonies, by the groom and the bride as well. Following this, the bride and groom may be asked by the rabbi to recite the following prayers:

Bride: O God, who has ordained marriage as the sanctification of the love of man and woman, I turn to Thee in prayer at this solemn moment. I thank Thee for him who is about to become my husband and for our love for each other. Enable me to be a worthy wife unto him. Grant that our marriage be marked by happiness and mutual devotion. As the veil is placed over my face, I accept it as a symbol of my devotion to my bridegroom. Amen.

Groom: O God, who has ordained marriage and sanctioned the love of man and woman, I turn to Thee in prayer at this solemn moment. I thank Thee for her who is about to become my wife and for our love for each other. Enable me to be a worthy husband unto her. Grant that our marriage be marked by happiness and mutual devotion. Even as I place this veil over my bride's face, so may my loving care encompass her in devotion and faithfulness. Amen.

The groom draws the veil over the bride's face, and those present recite the traditional blessing: "Our sister, be thou the mother of thousands of tens of thousands. May the Lord make you as Sarah, Rebekah, Rachel, and Leah." The ceremony may be concluded with the blessing of thanksgiving:

Blessed art Thou, O Lord our God, King of the Universe, who has kept us in life and sustained us and enabled us to celebrate this joyous occasion. (*Barukh ata adonai eloheinu melekh ha'olam shehebeyanu vekiyemanu vehigiyanu lazman hazeh.*)

YIHUD

This term refers to a private meeting of the bride and groom that takes place at Orthodox weddings immediately following the ceremony.

In the Jewish community of the past, the engaged couple were never permitted to be with each other without a chaperon. Immediately following the marriage ceremony, therefore, they were taken to a private room, where they could spend a brief period alone. This act of coming together as a married couple was called *Yihud*. It was actually a symbolic reminder that the marriage would not be consummated until the couple had been together in sexual union. Indeed, in a much earlier period, *Yihud* was the sexual union of the couple.

Though many couples who observe *Yihud* today do in fact see each other alone before the wedding, *Yihud* is still considered the true sign that the marriage rites have been completed properly.

The bride and groom spend a short period of time in a private room, where they break their fast with a light meal. In addition to affording them a brief period of privacy, it also enables them to rest and refresh themselves before joining their guests for the reception.

BLESSING OVER BREAD AND GRACE AFTER MEALS

Whenever Jews gather for a meal, it is customary to begin with the *Motzi*, the Blessing over Bread, and to conclude with Grace. At a wedding, the bread for blessing is frequently a large, braided *hallah*, which is placed on the bridal table.

A traditional *se'udat mitzvah* also includes the ritual of the washing of hands before breaking bread and before Grace is recited. It is customary to provide a pitcher and basin for washing hands before the meal, and finger bowls or a special dish for *mayim aharonim*, the washing after the meal.

The hosts generally provide small booklets which contain the blessings in Hebrew and in English. These may be purchased through a synagogue book shop, or at any Jewish book store. If desired, they may be especially ordered, well in advance, with the names of the couple and the marriage date imprinted on or inside the cover.

It is a great honor to be asked to lead the Grace (*Birkat Hamazon*) and the Wedding Blessings (*Sheva Berakhot*) following the wedding meal. The hosts may ask a member of either family, or the rabbi or cantor, to perform this function.

A special ritual is associated with the reciting of the Grace at a wedding. The leader raises a cup of wine, and leads the company in reciting the Grace. When the Grace is concluded, the cup of wine is put down, and a second cup is raised for the recital of the last six of the Wedding Blessings. Then the first cup is taken up again for the Blessing over Wine (which is also the first of the *Sheva Berakhot*). To conclude the ritual, the wine in both cups is mixed as a symbol of the union, and bride and groom sip from the wine.

The *Sheva Berakhot* may be recited after the Grace only if a *minyan*, at least ten adult males, is present. Seven different men may be asked to recite the seven blessings, which provides an opportunity for the hosts to honor any rabbis who may be present, as well as close relatives and friends. The hosts generally decide ahead of time who is to be honored with each blessing, and give a list to the leader.

THE SEVEN-DAY CELEBRATION

The tradition of a seven-day marriage celebration goes back to Biblical times. The Book of Judges refers to the "seven days of feasting" when Samson was married. These celebrations were marked by much feasting, music and dancing, the playing of games, and the telling of riddles. It is quite likely that many of the odes of the Song of Songs were composed as entertainment for such wedding feasts.

Legal sanction for the seven-day celebration is found in the *Shulḥan Arukh*, the code of Jewish law written in the sixteenth century: "He who espouses a maiden should rejoice with her seven days, and these are called the seven days of the repast. The groom should abstain from work, and he should not buy and sell in the marketplace, but he should eat and drink and rejoice with her."

The practice continues to this day, though it is now observed only by Hassidim and some non-Hassidic Orthodox Jews.

Friends and relatives of the bridal pair entertain them during the week following the wedding with special festive meals. If at least six new guests are present at each day's gathering, the *Sheva Berakhot* may be recited. At each meal, there is generally a discussion of verses from the Torah, as well as much merry-making, singing, and dancing.

TO EVERY THING THERE IS A SEASON, AND A TIME
TO EVERY PURPOSE UNDER THE HEAVEN. ECCLES.
3:1
—לכל זמן ועת לכל חפץ

THE procedures we have outlined up to this point are applicable to most Jewish weddings. However, variations must be introduced to help solve problems occasioned by special situations.

SECOND MARRIAGE

Wedding plans may present more than the usual complications when either member of the couple has been married previously. For this reason, a small wedding is considered most advisable. However, if it is the bride who is marrying for the first time, and if the groom has no children, she need not be deprived of the opportunity to have a large wedding with all the trimmings, if that is acceptable to her husband-to-be.

If the couple wish to entertain numerous friends and relatives, they may decide to hold the ceremony in the presence of only a few intimates and to follow it with a large reception, either immediately afterward or when they return from their honeymoon. In such a case, the ceremony could take place in the rabbi's study, in the home of the bride's parents, or even in the bride's own home.

If a large reception is not planned, the guests invited to the ceremony might also be invited for a luncheon or dinner afterward, either at home or at a hotel or restaurant. Careful plans for such a celebration in a public place can be made beforehand, so that it is as festive as it deserves to be.

When there is to be no reception at all, the bride or someone close to her can arrange for those present to drink a *Leḥayim* to the newlyweds immediately after the ceremony. Wine or champagne, small cakes, and perhaps hors d'oeuvres may be served.

Invitations, Announcements, Newspaper Announcements

For a small wedding, a handwritten note or telephone call is appropriate as an invitation. For a larger affair, either reception only or ceremony and reception, a formal invitation may be issued.

If the couple are to be married in the presence of only a few close friends and relatives, they will undoubtedly want to send announcements of the marriage to a wider circle.

An announcement of the marriage may also be sent to the newspaper, if the couple wish it.

Full details concerning the proper forms for invitations, announcements, and press announcements are found in Chapter III.

ATTENDANTS

A maid or matron of honor for the bride, and a best man for the groom are the usual attendants at a second marriage. Parents may serve in these capacities, as may older children of a widowed parent.

CHILDREN

A man or woman marrying for the second time is often concerned about a child or children of the first marriage. This concern is realistic, for almost no matter what their ages, children may feel deeply threatened and insecure at the prospect of a parent remarrying. Particularly in the case of a divorced parent, loyalty to the absent parent may cause a child considerable conflict.

It is suggested that the child himself be given the choice of whether or not to attend the wedding. To force him to attend against his wishes would certainly be unwise; it would be equally unwise to keep him away when he has expressed a desire to be part of this momentous event. Even if he does choose to be present, and appears happy about it, he may have a few bad moments. A close friend or relative, whom he knows well, may be a great source of comfort at this time, and could be asked to sit with him.

Because each situation is so different, it is difficult to formulate general rules. The wise and sensitive parent will gauge his child's feelings, and make decisions accordingly.

FORMER PARENTS-IN-LAW

When marriage is in the offing for a widowed parent, or for a divorced parent who has custody of the children, careful consideration should be given to the feelings of former in-laws.

As grandparents of the children, they are bound to be affected by a remarriage.

Though it is most unlikely that former in-laws would be invited to the wedding, a personal visit or telephone call to inform them of the event is extremely important. It might even be in order to suggest that they meet the fiancé, who ultimately will play such an important role in the lives of their grandchildren. The important thing to bear in mind is that the former in-laws have a difficult enough adjustment to make; being overlooked can only add to their unhappiness.

REMARRIAGE—WHEN?

A rabbi should always be consulted when remarriage is contemplated. Questions of religious law inevitably arise, and should be dealt with as early as possible.

In general, a widower does not remarry until the minimum, thirty-day period of mourning, *Sheloshim*, has passed. It is customary, however, to wait a full year, or at least until the passage of three Festivals (Pesaḥ, Shavuot, and Sukkot). Exceptions may be made in the case of a widower who was left with small children and who needs someone to care for them, or in the case of a widower without children, since he has not fulfilled the commandment to "be fruitful and multiply."

A widow or a divorcée is required by Jewish law to wait ninety days before marrying for a second time.

INTERMARRIAGE

The marriage of a Jew to a non-Jew is termed a mixed marriage. Such a marriage cannot be solemnized in the Jewish religion, for most rabbis will not officiate unless the non-Jewish party accepts Judaism through formal conversion. Once the person has converted, he is Jewish, and such a marriage is termed an intermarriage.

CONVERSION

Judaism does not seek converts, and in fact, rabbis generally try to dissuade would-be converts by indicating the hardships and problems involved in embracing Judaism. However, conversions do take place, most often in conjunction with marriage. The prospective convert would do well to see a rabbi as early as possible in order to discuss his intentions and to learn what obligations he must assume in the process of becoming a Jew.

The procedures for conversion vary in some details, depending on the affiliation of the rabbi. In all cases, a minimum period of study and preparation under the guidance of a rabbi or other qualified teacher is required. The course of study includes Bible, Jewish history, and religion, and whatever else the rabbi thinks appropriate. When the preparation is deemed adequate, a formal declaration is made before a *Bet Din*, or rabbinic tribunal, in which the convert renounces his former faith and affirms his belief in Judaism. He is then officially admitted as a member of the Jewish people, and receives a certificate of conversion. A Hebrew name is given to the convert to be used for religious purposes: usually Ruth or Sarah for a woman, Abraham or Judah for a man. The Hebrew name is used in the marriage contract (*ketubah*), on being called to the Torah, for special blessings, and so forth. It is not uncommon for a convert to adopt his new name for daily use as well. Because a convert is considered to be born anew, the new Hebrew name is followed by the phrase *Ben Avraham* (son of Abraham) or *Bat Avraham* (daughter of Abraham), thus linking the convert with the first Jew, the Patriarch Abraham.

Conversion by Orthodox and Conservative rabbis also requires circumcision and ritual immersion for the male convert, and ritual immersion for the female convert.

A convert to Judaism is recognized as a full member of the Jewish community. Jews are fond of recalling that the Biblical Ruth was a convert, and that her great-grandson was King David, the "sweet singer of Israel."

THE WEDDING OF A CONVERT

When a Jew marries a non-Jew who has accepted Judaism through formal conversion, it is considered an occasion of serious moment. In addition to all the normal problems and decisions entailed in getting married, the convert has undergone a difficult period of soul-searching before making a final commitment. It is quite likely that such a marriage will be marked by a greater degree of solemnity than is usual.

The couple may prefer a small, intimate wedding to which only the families and close friends will be invited. There may, however, be circumstances in which the acceptance of the convert by the Jewish family and by the community can be eased by having a large wedding. The presence of congregational and community leaders demonstrates warm acceptance of the newcomer's place as a member of the Jewish people.

The act of conversion to Judaism does not sever the relationship of the convert to his parents or other members of his family. The convert's family must be made to feel welcome and comfortable at the wedding. They should be briefed in advance about the rituals of the ceremony and everything that is to take place. Knowing what to expect and what is expected of them will help put them at ease.

The officiating rabbi decides whether or not the convert's parents may escort him down the aisle. Orthodox rabbis generally do not permit it, in which case someone else must be designated as escort. If the groom is the convert, his best man may escort him; if it is the bride, some member of the groom's family may assume this position. Sometimes, though the rabbi permits the convert's parents to escort him to the canopy, the parents themselves prefer not to participate in the ceremony of a religion that is not their own. In this case, they should be seated in the first row before the processional begins. It would then be considerate for the Jewish parents to forego standing under the *ḥuppah*, and to take seats in the first row after escorting their child down the aisle. Both sets of parents would participate in the recessional and, needless to say, both sets of parents stand in the receiving line after the ceremony to greet their guests and receive their good wishes.

CIVIL MARRIAGE

All religious groups in Judaism disapprove of civil marriage. Marriage is a sacred event, and it must be solemnized in a religious ceremony as prescribed by Jewish law and tradition. If a couple have been married by civil authorities, every effort is made to persuade them to validate the marriage by a religious ceremony.

Nevertheless, from the legal viewpoint, the couple married in a civil ceremony are regarded as husband and wife. Should the marriage be dissolved, Orthodox and Conservative rabbis will, for the most part, require a *get*, a religious divorce, and will not officiate at a remarriage of either partner unless such a decree has been obtained. The children of a civil marriage are regarded as legitimate, and are entitled to participate in the various rites and rituals of the Jewish religion.

In the eyes of the religious community, however, the civil marriage is considered a repudiation both of Jewish law and of Jewish sentiment.

WEDDING OF A RABBI OR MEMBER OF A RABBI'S FAMILY

When a rabbi or a member of a rabbi's family marries, the problems involved in deciding what kind of wedding to have and whom to invite may be complicated by the presence of the congregation. The members of the synagogue play an important role in the life of the rabbi. If he has served the congregation for a long time, many intimate relationships have been established. Whether or not he invites the entire congregation may well depend on his length of service, but this in itself is not necessarily decisive. Marriage is, after all, a personal matter, and congregations generally understand this. Perhaps the most important consideration is the attitude of the rabbi's bride-to-be or, as the case may be, the rabbi's child who is about to be married. A public wedding is not to everyone's taste by any means, and a rabbi and his family are surely entitled to privacy, if they want it!

There are many ways of handling the wedding of a rabbi or a member of his family, and the following suggestions may prove helpful. When the wedding is to take place in the rabbi's own synagogue or in a synagogue in the same city, he may: invite the entire congregation to the ceremony and reception (the reception may run the gamut from champagne and petits fours to a full, sit-down dinner); invite the entire congregation to the ceremony only; or invite the entire congregation to the reception only. If an invitation to the entire membership is out of the question, the list might be limited to official representatives of the various congregational organizations. The wedding could also be small, with the immediate families and close friends present and no congregational representation.

When the wedding is to take place in another city, the rabbi may still wish to invite personal friends and some official representatives from his congregation. If he himself is the groom, the *Aufruf* (see Chapter VIII) may be held in his own synagogue, and he may be the host at the *kiddush* after service.

A congregation may wish to celebrate the marriage of its rabbi with a reception to be held either before or after the wedding date. It might follow a Friday night or Saturday morning service, or could take the form of an especially festive *kiddush* for the rabbi's *Aufruf*.

Here are two sample invitations to such receptions:

> *Congregation B'nai Sholom*
> *takes pleasure in inviting you to a reception*
> *in honor of*
> *Rabbi and Mrs. Simon Berk*
> *on the occasion of their recent marriage*
> *Saturday, September 12, 1966*
> *following the Sabbath service*
> *100 Hempstead Avenue   Rockville Centre, N.Y.*

> *You are cordially invited*
> *to a reception in honor of*
> *Rabbi Simon Berk*
> *and*
> *Miss Sharon Sternberg*
> *on the occasion of their forthcoming marriage*
> *Sunday, June 12, 1966*
> *at three o'clock*
> *Temple B'nai Sholom*
> *Rockville Centre*

GIFTS TO THE RABBI

Wedding gifts to a rabbi and his wife may be sent by the congregation as a whole, as well as by the sisterhood, the men's club, and other organizations. Individual members may, of course, elect to send personal gifts.

An official gift might be a fine ceremonial object, a painting, an important set of books, or something in silver. It is thoughtful to consult the rabbi and his wife before making the final selection.

Who Officiates?

If the rabbi is being married in his own synagogue, he invites a close friend, a neighboring rabbi, or an older colleague to officiate. When the wedding takes place in the synagogue of the bride's family, her rabbi officiates perhaps together with another rabbi who is close to the groom.

The rabbi whose son or daughter is marrying plays a dual role, but it can be done with relative ease. If the wedding is in his own synagogue, he is the chief officiant; if the wedding takes place elsewhere, he officiates together with the rabbi of that synagogue. It is customary, however, for the host rabbi to offer the rabbi-father complete freedom to conduct the ceremony as he wishes.

In his role as father, the rabbi may join his wife to escort their child to the *ḥuppah*. When they reach the canopy, the rabbi takes his place as officiant and his wife stands near their child. When the ceremony is concluded, the rabbi joins his wife for the recessional. The rabbi who customarily wears a clerical robe to officiate will probably not wish to do so at the marriage of his child. His role as father is the most important one on this occasion, and he should wear whatever dress is appropriate to the style of the wedding.

Rabbi's Gifts for Officiating Clergy

When a rabbi invites a colleague to officiate at his wedding, he thanks him afterward with a cordial letter and perhaps a gift. The cantor who officiates should be thanked in similar fashion.

The above suggestions may, in general, serve as a guide for the marriages of cantors, other members of a synagogue staff, and their families.

ELOPEMENT

For a couple to marry in opposition to their parents' will, or even without the presence of parents, is a relatively unusual occurrence in Jewish life, and one that is not viewed favorably. The rabbi to whom the couple come will question them most carefully, and will hesitate to solemnize the marriage unless he is convinced beyond any doubt that it is desirable. He may even insist that the parents be notified of what is about to take place before proceeding.

For purely technical reasons, too, a Jewish elopement is not easy. Two witnesses must be present, and it may be necessary to call in additional forces to hold the *huppah.* Some Orthodox rabbis will only officiate in the presence of a *minyan.*

Having indicated the difficulties that stand in the way of a Jewish elopement, it must be stated that there are situations in which it is the only solution to a problem, and that such elopements do occasionally occur. The ceremony usually takes place in the rabbi's study or home in the presence of two witnesses and whoever else may be needed.

Formal announcements of the marriage may be issued, if possible in the name of the bride's parents. An acceptable alternative would be a small card:

Miss Anne Cohen   Mr. David Geld
Married
January 5, 1965

WHEN PLANS HAVE TO BE CHANGED

IN TIME OF DEATH

In the event that a death occurs in either family, and the wedding date falls during the period of *shivah* (the first seven days), the wedding must be postponed. If the wedding date occurs during *sheloshim* (the first thirty days), then the marriage takes place after the conclusion of *sheloshim.* Usually, as a sign of mourning, the wedding is small, with only closest family and friends present. The festivities are subdued.

Circumstances may call for other procedures. There have been situations in which promises were made to the departed one to hold the wedding as originally planned. In all cases it is wise to consult a rabbi before making any decisions.

IN TIME OF ILLNESS

The serious illness of a close relative of the bride or groom may call for some changes in the wedding plans. Though postponement may appear to be the logical course of action, it may not always be the best procedure. The patient himself may insist that plans proceed as scheduled, or that the wedding take place on the appointed day, perhaps the only change being to limit the number of guests. It may be desirable to advance the wedding date, or even to hold the marriage at the patient's bedside. The patient's happiness and well-being should be of primary concern in determining how best to proceed. Consultation with the attending physician and with the rabbi is, of course, essential.

NOTIFYING GUESTS

If invitations to the wedding have already been sent, it is necessary to advise those on the guest list that plans have been changed. If time permits, a card should be printed and mailed as quickly as possible. If there is not sufficient time, guests should be notified by telephone or telegram. On occasion, particularly if prominent families are involved, a notice in the newspapers may be called for.

Postponement. A widespread superstition holds that it is bad luck to postpone a wedding, but there is absolutely nothing in Jewish law to support this. If postponement is necessary, guests should be so notified, with an indication of the new date, if that has been set:

Mr. and Mrs. Julian Greenberg announce that the marriage of their daughter Jean to Saul Berger has been postponed.

Mr. and Mrs. Julian Greenberg announce that the marriage of their daughter has been postponed from Sunday, the eighteenth of December to Sunday, the fourth of February
at five o'clock
Temple Emanuel
New York City
R.S.V.P.

Recalling an Invitation. Any of a number of possible occurrences may make it necessary to recall a wedding invitation. Suitable announcements are suggested below, but it should be understood that any appropriate wording may be used.

The wedding is canceled
Mr. and Mrs. Jack Green announce that the marriage of their daughter, Sandra, to Mr. Sidney Roth, will not take place.

Death in the Family

Mrs. Moses Abrahams regrets that the death of her husband, Moses Abrahams, ע״ה obliges her to recall the invitation to the wedding of her daughter.

NOTE: The Hebrew abbreviation is for the phrase *Alav Hashalom*, "May he rest in peace," or for a woman, *Aleha Hashalom*.

Illness in the Family

Owing to the illness of Mrs. Benjamin Isaacson, Mr. and Mrs. Adam Davidowitz wish to recall the invitation to the wedding of their daughter, Leah, to Mr. Joseph Isaacson.

If the couple is married privately following the recall of an invitation to a wedding, announcements of the marriage may be issued.

Groom in the Service. If the groom is called to army duty after wedding invitations have been sent out, plans may have to be altered. If it is decided to hold the wedding *en famille* at an earlier date, a suitable announcement would be:

Mr. and Mrs. William Chanin wish to recall the invitation to the wedding of their daughter, Helen, to Mr. Jeremy Stein, owing to his having been called for military service. The couple will be married privately, at an earlier date.

BROKEN ENGAGEMENTS

Broken engagements do occur, and the experience can be exceedingly painful. Those concerned will want to take care of the necessary social obligations as quickly as possible, and to consider the entire matter a closed book. Certainly, recriminations or prolonged discussions of the reasons for the break-up can serve no useful purpose.

The termination of an engagement may be announced in the newspapers, especially if the principals are prominent, or if the wedding date is near at hand:

Mr. and Mrs. Herman Ginzberg announce that the engagement of their daughter, Susan, to Mr. Charles Kay, has been terminated by mutual consent.

If such an announcement is not called for, the news is spread by word of mouth.

The engagement ring and any other gifts that the couple may have given each other are returned. All gifts received from others, including shower or wedding gifts, must be returned as well. The engaged girl, perhaps with her mother's assistance, sends a polite note of explanation with each gift.

X
A
GUIDE
FOR
GUESTS

O FRIENDS OF THE WEDDED PAIR,
HASTE NOW TO DRINK THE WINE OF
FRIENDSHIP FROM THE BOWL OF JOY.

MOSES IBN EZRA

The person who receives an invitation to a wedding is expected, in the words of the Wedding Blessings, to "make glad the heart of the bridegroom and the bride." This means not only joining in the festivities with enthusiasm, but also fulfilling certain social responsibilities promptly and considerately.

ACCEPTING THE INVITATION

An invitation should be acknowledged as soon as possible after its receipt. Even if no reply is requested, a note to the hosts telling whether or not you plan to attend is gracious.

ANSWERING THE FORMAL INVITATION

The accepted form for replying to a formal, engraved invitation is a note handwritten on a double sheet of stationery, with the writing on the first page. The wording of the note follows the style of the invitation itself:

> Mr. and Mrs. Theodore Sacks
> accept with pleasure
> the kind invitation of
> Mr. and Mrs. Schneider
> to the marriage of their daughter
> on Sunday, the twentieth of June
> at five o'clock
> at Temple Israel

A regret is worded in similar fashion:

> Mr. and Mrs. Emanuel Frank
> regret that they are unable to accept
> Mr. and Mrs. Schneider's
> kind invitation to the wedding of
> their daughter
> on Sunday, the twentieth of June

The exact wording need not be adhered to rigidly, as long as the general style is followed. A reply of regret at being unable to attend may give the reason:

Mr. and Mrs. Emanuel Frank
regret that owing to a prior engagement
they are unable to accept . . .

If close friends and relatives feel uncomfortable with such formality, there is no reason why they should not respond with a personal note.

If a printed response card is enclosed with the invitation, the guest simply inserts the names of those who will or will not attend.

ANSWERING THE INFORMAL INVITATION

The reply to an informal invitation follows the form in which the invitation is received. Response by telephone or telegram is correct. If the invitation is printed or handwritten, the reply is a personal note to the hosts:

Dear Hadassah and George,
Saul and I accept with pleasure your kind invitation to Dorothy's wedding on June 20th. We look forward to being with you.
Fondest regards and *Mazal Tov*.

Yours,
Dora Solomon

Dear Mr. and Mrs. Schneider,
We were delighted to receive the invitation to Dorothy's wedding. Unfortunately, we will not be able to be with you, because Bobby's graduation is taking place on that day.
Please accept our best wishes for the future happiness of the couple.

Cordially,
Eva and Barry Lee

UNMARRIED GUESTS

An unmarried man or woman should not embarrass the hosts by asking permission to bring a friend or fiancé to the wedding if that person has not been invited.

THE ANNOUNCEMENT

A wedding announcement imposes no obligations; neither a response nor a gift is required. If this seems unfriendly to you, a warm note of good wishes or even a gift may be dispatched, with no fear whatsoever of offending good taste.

TELEGRAMS

If you are unable to attend a wedding to which you have been invited, sending a telegram is a splendid way to gladden the hearts of the bride and groom. A telegram may also be sent by a friend or relative to a very small wedding at which only the immediate families of the couple are present.

The telegram should be sent early on the day of the wedding to the bride's home or to the wedding locale. It may be addressed to the new couple or to whichever set of parents you are close to.

Originality and humor in a telegram are fine, if the message really is original and humorous. Generally, a simple and sincere message is more appropriate. Among Jews it is customary to wish the couple and their families, "*Mazal Tov*," or "Good luck and congratulations"; and the parents, "May you have much *nahes* (joy)."

WEDDING PRESENTS

Whether or not to give a wedding present is often a vexing question, but there are some simple guidelines to follow.

If you accept a wedding invitation, it is customary to send a present. If you do not attend the wedding, you may still wish to give the couple a gift, but it is not obligatory. If you are not invited to the wedding, particularly if it is small, you may wish to send a present simply out of affection for the couple or their families. In this instance, be guided by your own instincts and your knowledge of the people involved.

Wedding gifts should be sent before the wedding to the bride at her home. If you cannot manage this, the gift may be sent to the couple after the wedding at their home. It is in poor taste to bring a gift, even if it fits into an envelope, to the wedding itself. Your personal card, with or without a message, accompanies the gift.

A wedding gift may be anything that you think will please the couple. It will be most appreciated if it is selected with their tastes and needs in mind. Many brides choose china and silver patterns, which they list in the bridal registry of a local store.

A gift of either, even one small piece, will surely be welcome. You might also select glassware or an accessory for her table that will fit nicely with her patterns.

While silver is considered a traditional gift, many young couples prefer an informal style of living, and may be happier with contemporary designs in wood, stainless steel, or pottery.

A monetary gift in the form of a check or securities is almost always welcome, and at times may be the only answer if you do not know what to give. A cordial note should, of course, accompany the gift.

GIFTS FOR THE JEWISH HOME

A ceremonial object, a book or picture on a Jewish theme, or an item of Israeli handicraft makes an excellent gift for a Jewish couple, and the possibilities are extensive. Many of these items can be purchased through the gift-and-book shop run by the sisterhood of a local synagogue, or at stores specializing in these items. Any of the following would be appropriate gifts:

Candlesticks	*Havdalah* spice box
(preferably silver or brass)	*Seder* plate
Hanukah *menorah*	*Mezuzah*
Kiddush cup	Bible
Hallah tray	Haggadah
Hallah knife	

Sometimes a silver wine goblet is given by a close friend or relative with a suggestion that it be used at the wedding ceremony. If the couple do not already have a *kiddush* cup designated for this purpose, such a gift becomes doubly meaningful. The donor may wish to have the cup suitably engraved with the wedding date and the names or monogram of the bride and groom.

WHAT TO WEAR

A wedding guest owes it to his hosts to consider carefully what he or she will wear. It is an honor to be invited to a wedding, and the appearance of the guests is an integral part of the picture. Good taste and appropriateness are the primary criteria; this leaves ample opportunity for individual expression, but within a specified framework. The following is a brief guide to appropriate wedding attire. Note that daytime usually means before five o'clock.

Formal Daytime Wedding. Men: Cutaway or dark sack coat with striped trousers, or a dark suit, white shirt, black shoes. Women: Street-length cocktail dress or suit, in a simple style and never décolleté; small veil or hat, gloves and small bag. Black is acceptable.

Informal Daytime Wedding. Men: Dark suit, white shirt, black shoes. Women: Simply-styled, but dressy, street-length dress or suit; small hat or veil; gloves and small bag.

Formal Evening Wedding. Men: White tie and tails or dinner jacket. Women: Short or long evening dress, small veil, gloves and bag.

Informal Evening Wedding. Men: Dark suit, white shirt, black shoes. Women: Short cocktail dress or suit, in a simple style, small hat or veil, gloves and bag.

No matter where the wedding takes place, the ceremony is a religious one. Women wearing low-cut gowns are advised to wear stoles or jackets during the ceremony. Sometimes the invitation to an Orthodox wedding specifically requests female guests to "Please wear appropriate dress," and this usually means a decorous dress, with sleeves, and a head covering.

At Orthodox and Conservative weddings, and at times at Reform weddings, men are expected to keep their heads covered. In the synagogue, a street hat may be worn, but it is more usual to don a skullcap, either one's own or one provided by the hosts.

Synagogue Manners

There is no such thing as coming fashionably late to a wedding. The only time it might be excusable is when a buffet reception precedes the ceremony, a practice in some large cities. The invitation does not always make clear that the time stated is for the preceremony reception, which may go on for an hour or more. If it is important for you to know whether a reception is taking place first, call the synagogue or hotel where the wedding is to be held.

Most often, the time stated on the invitation is for the start of the ceremony. Try to arrive ten to fifteen minutes early. You will probably be greeted by an usher. If you are not known to him, tell him who you are, "I'm a friend of the bride," or "I'm a cousin of the groom," and let him show you to a seat.

If a man and woman enter together, the usher may offer his arm to the woman. The man then walks behind. If you have to choose your own seat, be guided by the fact that the first few rows are generally for family. At Orthodox weddings, men and women may be separated, but you will probably be advised of this when you enter.

Once seated, remain in your place. Conversation is permitted before the processional starts, but should be low and kept to a minimum.

If you come with a young child, try to sit at the rear of the sanctuary or on the aisle to assure an unobtrusive getaway, if necessary. By the way, youngsters should be brought to a wedding only if specifically invited.

AT THE RECEPTION

At the receiving line, greet the members of the bridal party briefly, introducing yourself to those who may not know you. A few words of warm congratulations are sufficient; if you have more to say or news to tell, you will find an opportunity later on. In the event that you plan to leave early, explain this to your hosts and indicate that you will slip out quietly so as not to disturb them.

A wedding reception is a celebration—enjoy it. Your hosts will be happy if they see that you feel comfortable and are mingling with the other guests. Formal introductions among guests at a wedding are unnecessary; treat the situation as if you were at a party in the hosts' home.

Let yourself be caught up in the festivities. When asked to pose for a photograph, do so graciously. If a *horah* or other folk dance is started, don't just be an observer. Anyone can join in; it's fun!

If a toast is made and you are not fond of the drink offered or do not drink alcoholic beverages, just raise your glass of water or pretend to drink what has been served you.

If the Grace after Meals is recited, participate if you are able, otherwise sit quietly out of deference to the others. Frequently the Grace book has an English translation, which you may read silently if you cannot follow the Hebrew. It is extremely impolite, of course, to leave the table during the recital of the Grace.

When you are ready to leave, say your good-bys to the bride and groom and to the hosts, whom you thank for having invited you. If you are a close friend or relative of the parents of either bride or groom, drop them a note or telephone them after a few days have passed to let them know how much you enjoyed being at their *simḥa*.

GUEST WITH SPECIAL DIET

A guest whose health requires that he follow a strict diet, or one who eats only kosher food and knows that it will be a nonkosher reception, will feel more comfortable—and his hosts will, too—if he informs them beforehand, so that proper arrangements can be made. It is usually a simple matter for the hosts to provide special food for him.

If the guest does not know whether kosher food is to be served, and prefers not to ask the hosts, he can obtain the information by calling the hotel or hall where the wedding will take place.

THE GUEST IN MOURNING

A person who has sustained a recent loss of a close relative generally does not attend a wedding during the period of *shivah*, the first week. If he is very close to the bride or groom, he may attend a wedding during *sheloshim*, the first thirty days, but will leave immediately after the ceremony. After the thirty-day period has passed, he may attend the reception as well, but may decide to refrain from participating in the dancing.

A woman in mourning who attends a wedding during the first thirty days wears a dark or very simple dress without adornment.

THE OUT-OF-TOWN GUEST

Unless accommodations for an overnight stay are being arranged by the hosts, you should make your hotel arrangements well ahead of time. If you arrive the day of the wedding, or the day before, bear in mind that the preparations for the wedding may be so hectic that you may have to wait until the wedding to see the family. A telephone call, however, would be in order.

ADVICE FOR THE NON-JEWISH GUEST

There are no special requirements for a non-Jewish guest at a Jewish wedding. Your hosts will appreciate your observing the same behavior as the Jewish guests, including the wearing of a skullcap when this is called for.

XI

MR. and MRS.

BY WISDOM IS A HOUSE BUILDED AND
BY UNDERSTANDING IT IS ESTABLISHED.
PROVERBS 24:3

The ancient rabbis found an important lesson in the Hebrew words for man and wife. Man is *ish* and wife is *isha*—almost alike, but not quite. The letters that make the difference are *yod* and *hei*, which together form *Yah*, one of the names of God.

The lesson is clear. Marriage is a compact in which there are not two partners, but three—man, woman, and God. When man and woman are joined together and live in peace and harmony, God is in their midst.

Before ringing down the curtain on your wedding, may we have a last word with you, Mr. and Mrs. ———? Important as the wedding itself may be, it is merely the prelude to your new life as a married couple. You are now the principal actors in an exciting adventure, and your skill and wisdom will be tested as never before. From now on, all the major decisions that will affect your future happiness will have to be made by you, and you alone.

We will not attempt to advise you on the problems of personal relationships that arise in every marriage. You will find guidance in these matters in the many excellent marriage manuals that are available. We are concerned, however, with one important decision that every Jewish couple should make at the very outset of their marriage. What kind of Jewish home will you have?

There is no one acceptable definition of what makes a home Jewish, beyond the fact that Jews live there. Judaism has many facets, and the Jewish community is characterized by as many different views and practices, all legitimately Jewish. In our society, Jews are free to select those aspects of Jewish life that have meaning for them; or they are free to select none, and to lead a life lacking in any specific Jewish expression.

If you are among those who wish to weave a design of Jewish living in your home, there are many patterns to choose from. The religious pattern offers rich possibilities. In the traditional home, there is, first and foremost, the system of the dietary laws, or *kashrut*. If you were brought up in a kosher home, you will have no difficulty setting up your kitchen in accordance with the rules. Chances are that your mother will be delighted to help.

If, however, you have had little experience with *kashrut*, but have decided, for your own good reasons, to have a kosher home, the best procedure is to consult a rabbi. He will be able to instruct you in the basic rules and in the religious significance of this historic observance. On page 165, you will find the names of several publications that deal with the dietary laws.

In the homes of religious Jews of the three groups there will be all or some of the various ritual and ceremonial objects: the Sabbath and Festival candlesticks, the *kiddush* cup, the wine decanter, the *hallah* cover and knife, the *Havdalah* spice box and braided candle, the Passover *seder* plate, the Hanukah *menorah*, the cup of Elijah, and others. All of these objects are beautiful, visual reminders of the cycle of the Jewish year. They are used throughout a lifetime, and are generally among the most cherished possessions in the home. In some homes they are heirlooms and are passed from one generation to another. In others, emphasis may be placed on their artistic merit, and the owners may take great pride in acquiring more than one of a ceremonial object. As children are born, additional *kiddush* cups, candlesticks, and other items may be added.

Undoubtedly, the best known of all Jewish ritual objects is the *mezuzah*, which is attached to the doorpost of the home. The *mezuzah* comes in various shapes and designs and contains a little parchment scroll on which is inscribed a passage from the Torah (Deuteronomy 6:4–9 and 11:13–21). The *mezuzah* gives character to the home even before you enter: it is a Jewish home.

There are many other objects, useful and ornamental, which add to the Jewish character of a home. Art and music can provide some of them. No one is quite sure what Jewish art or Jewish music is, but theoretical questions aside, there are many works by Jewish and Israeli artists that have an unmistakably Jewish flavor. In the field of music, you can choose from a wide selection of recordings of sacred and folk music in Hebrew, Yiddish, and English, and these certainly add to the Jewish atmosphere of the home.

Someone has said, "If you want to know the interests of the people who live in a home, look at the bookshelves." Jews, by and large, have inherited a love of books, and most of them have libraries in their homes. The religious home will have, as essentials, the Bible and several prayerbooks. Generally, the Jewish bookshelf will include some of the great classics of Jewish literature (most of them now available in English): Mishna, Talmud, Midrash, Zohar, *Shulḥan Arukh* (Code of Jewish Law), the works of Maimonides, books on the Bible, Jewish history, biography, literature, philosophy, and theology. A handy, one-volume Jewish encyclopedia can prove useful. Membership in the Jewish Publication Society will provide the interested reader with great Jewish works of the past as well as contemporary works. If an Anglo-Jewish newspaper is published in your area, make sure it finds its way into your home. You will also probably want to subscribe to at least one of the Jewish magazines, which are published by the various national organizations. Such publications are indispensable to a Jew who wants to relate to current Jewish life and thought.

A Jewish home does not exist in isolation from its neighbors, and a Jewish couple will discover soon enough that they are part of a community with which they will be expected to identify. The great sage Hillel said, "Separate not thyself from the community," and his words are an axiom of Jewish life. You will have to make many decisions. Shall we join a synagogue? Which one? Many national and local organizations will ask you to become members; Jewish charities will seek contributions. You may open the doors of your home to let the community in, or you may keep them closed and shut it out, but it is important to remember that the establishment of a Jewish home means relating in a positive way to the community, to some aspect of Jewish life.

We have been talking about those elements in the home which make it distinctively Jewish, but the decisive test of a Jewish home lies in its universal qualities, in the things that we share with our neighbors of all faiths. Jews are members of the broader community around them, and they share in its concerns. If the teachings of Judaism are to be meaningful, they must be applied to the important issues and problems of our society.

The ideal Jewish home is one in which there is *shalom bayit*, an atmosphere of peace and harmony. It is a home in which people respect each other as individuals, husband and wife, parent and child, sister and brother. It is a home in which great, moral virtues are taught more by example than by precept, and where the joy of living is found in shared tasks and responsibilities.

We hope this will be your home, and we wish you every happiness in your new life.

Glossary

All words are Hebrew, unless otherwise noted. For the most part, they are transliterated as pronounced in modern, Israeli Hebrew. Note that both "ḥ" (the Hebrew letter *ḥet*) and *kh* (the Hebrew letter *khof*) are pronounced like the German *ch* in *ach*.

Aliyah Literally, "going up" or "ascent." The honor of being called up to the reading of the Torah.

Aufruf (German; popularly known in Yiddish as *Ufruf*) The ceremony of calling the bridegroom to the reading of the Torah before his wedding day.

Badeken (Yiddish) The ceremony prior to the actual marriage ceremony, in which the groom draws the veil over the bride's face.

Badḥen (Yiddish pronunciation; in Hebrew, *badḥan*) A jester or bard.

Bet Din A rabbinic court.

Bimah The platform before the ark.

Birkat Hamazon Grace after Meals.

Brit Milah (Also *bris*) Ceremony of circumcision.

Eirusin Betrothal.

"El Malei Raḥamim" "O Lord, full of compassion." The opening words of the Memorial Prayer for the Dead.

Get The divorce document.

Haftarah The selection from the Prophets read after the reading from the Torah.

Ḥalitzah The ritual absolving a childless widow of the obligation to marry her dead husband's brother (as prescribed by the Levirate law of marriage).

Ḥallah The loaf of bread eaten on Sabbaths, Festivals, and special occasions.

Ḥatan (Also, *ḥossen*) Bridegroom.

Havdalah The ceremony marking the conclusion of the Sabbath.

Horah A popular folk dance in Israel.

Ḥuppah The marriage canopy.

Kallah Bride.

Kashrut (From which comes the adjective *kasher*, or kosher) The dietary laws.

Ketubah The marriage contract.

Kiddush Literally, "sanctification." The name given to the blessing over ritual wine, and also to the light refreshments that may be served with wine, following a synagogue service.

Kittel (Yiddish) A white robe worn by men on sacred occasions.

Kohen A priest. Any descendant of the ancient priestly class.

Leḥayim "To life." A popular toast.

Ma'asim Tovim "Good deeds."

Mahatonim (Yiddish pronunciation; in Hebrew, *meḥutanim*) Relatives by marriage.

Mashgiakh A ritual supervisor.

Mazal Tov "Good luck." Used also as congratulations.

Menorah The eight-branched candelabrum used during Ḥanukah.

Mesader Kiddushin One who solemnizes a marriage.

Mezuzah A piece of parchment containing verses from the Book of Leviticus, which is inserted in a case and affixed to the doorpost of a house.

Mikvah A ritual bath.

Minyan The quorum of ten adult males required for many religious ceremonies.

Mitzvah Literally, "commandment." Commonly used to mean a good deed, one that is in fulfillment of a sacred duty.

Mizbei'ah An altar.

Motzi The name given to the Blessing over Bread, from the concluding words of the blessing, *hamotzi leḥem min ha'aretz*, "He who brings forth bread from the earth."

Naḥes (Yiddish pronunciation; in Hebrew, *naḥat*) Pleasure, joy.

Nisu'in Marriage.

Pareve (Yiddish) Neutral. Describes foods that are neither meat nor dairy.

Se'udah A meal.

Se'udat Mitzvah A meal following the fulfillment of a religious duty.

Shadḥan A matchmaker.

Sheloshim Literally, "thirty." The first thirty days of mourning.

Sheva Berakhot The Seven Wedding Blessings.

Shivah Literally, "seven." The first week of mourning.

Simḥa A joyous occasion.

Tallit (Also, *tallis*) A prayer shawl.

Tena'im Literally, "conditions." The traditional betrothal ceremony, or the betrothal agreement.

Yarmulkes (Yiddish) Skullcaps.

Yiḥud The ceremony immediately following the marriage ceremony, in which the bride and groom are alone together for the first time as man and wife.

Books for Further Reading
and Reference

The Jewish Marriage Anthology, by Philip and Hanna Goodman. The Jewish Publication Society of America. A thoroughly rewarding collection of quotations, essays, stories, poems, articles, and photographs.

The Lifetime of a Jew, by Hayyim Schauss. Union of American Hebrew Congregations. Colorful description of the history and development of marriage and other important ceremonies and rituals.

Across the Threshold, A Guide for the Jewish Homemaker, by Shonie B. Levi and Sylvia R. Kaplan. Farrar, Straus and Cudahy, and the National Women's League. Available in a paperback edition under the title, *Guide for the Jewish Homemaker*, published by Schocken Books. A comprehensive guide to Sabbath and holiday observance, and every aspect of the Jewish home.

A Marriage Manual, by Hannah and Abraham Stone. Simon and Schuster. A highly recommended text on sexual relations in marriage.

Jewish Family Life—The Duty of the Woman, a pamphlet by Rabbi Sidney B. Hoenig. Published by The Spero Foundation and available through the Union of Orthodox Jewish Congregations of America. Comprehensive treatment of the Jewish laws governing sexual relations in marriage.

A Hedge of Roses, Jewish Insights into Marriage and Married Life, by Norman Lamm. Philipp Feldheim, Inc. A sensitive interpretation of the traditional, Orthodox view of marriage.

The Dietary Laws, Their Meaning for Our Time, a pamphlet by Rabbi Samuel H. Dresner and Rabbi Seymour Siegel. Burning Bush Press.

Kashruth, Union of Orthodox Jewish Congregations of America. (A pamphlet on the dietary laws.)

The New Settlement Cook Book, by Mrs. Simon Kander. Simon and Schuster.

Jewish Festival Cook Book, by Fanny Engle and Gertrude Blair. Paperback Library.

The Israeli Cook Book, by Molly Bar-David. Crown.

Index